April 18, 1975
Station WFTL, Ft. Lau-
derdale, Florida, is on
the air. A discussion pro-
gram is in progress. Its
subject is

THE BERMUDA TRIANGLE.

Ray Smithers, the host, is awaiting questions from the radio audience, but no call can get through. All nine telephone lines have gone dead. Suddenly one line opens. An authoritative voice booms this message:

- Every living thing on this planet has an aura.
- The area you are now discussing is the aura of this planet.
- It is the communicative channel through which the Millionth Counsel governs this planet.
- Those entering this area when the channel is open do not disappear. They are in the timeless void and are alive and well.

The source of the message could not be determined. The freak breakdown and the strange phone call were beyond coincidence. Had the world really been informed of the facts behind the SECRETS OF THE BERMUDA TRIANGLE? This incident and hundreds of others prompt the speculation and the theory that will grow more and more plausible as you turn the pages of this intriguing new book!

SECRETS OF THE BERMUDA TRIANGLE

by Alan Landsburg

WARNER BOOKS

A Warner Communications Company

WARNER BOOKS EDITION

Copyright © 1978 by Ahmel, Inc. of California
All rights reserved

ISBN 0-446-89626-8

Warner Books, Inc., 75 Rockefeller Plaza, New York, N.Y. 10019

Ⓦ A Warner Communications Company

Printed in the United States of America

Not associated with Warner Press, Inc. of Anderson, Indiana

First Printing: June, 1978

10 9 8 7 6 5 4 3 2 1

SECRETS
OF THE
BERMUDA
TRIANGLE

CHAPTER ONE

Message from Space

The world over, phone-in TV and radio programs know how to handle oddballs. Day and night, the bores, the drunks, the pompous, the facetious, and the plain nutty are intercepted and fended off by the host or the station with a smoothness that comes from long years of experience. So what happened to Ray Smithers of WFTL radio in Fort Lauderdale, Florida, on the night of April 13, 1975 was of a different dimension—literally.

He took a call on the show that not only broke all the rules, but all the equipment, as well. It came from a source that has never been identified and whose message is so cryptic that even now it cannot be fully understood. Yet it may be one of the key statements, a crucial clue, in a new investigation of what remains the world's greatest contemporary mystery—just what is going on in that mystifyingly perilous area known as the Bermuda Triangle? Is there a fundamental, undiscovered secret that has led to all those well-documented deaths, disasters, and disappearances? If so, how near are we to finding out the nature of this secret?

The scene in the WFTL studio had just that element of strangeness, of inexplicable events taking place in humdrum surroundings, that marks so many of the incidents in the area. Sitting at the control desk, nine telephone lines to the outside world in front of him, was Ray Smithers, a man well-known locally as a sensible and reassuring personality, and Program Director for the sister station WGLO. On this night he was joining WFTL as co-host of a program about the Bermuda Triangle, originally scheduled as six two-hour specials, but then increased to three hours each because of the massive audience reaction. "In twenty years' experience I've never known such a response," he says now. The phones were jammed solid throughout every transmission. The guest in the studio for that particular program was Page Bryant, from Chicago, a psychic who had made a deep study of the Triangle mystery under 18 hours of hypnosis and written a book about it, *Psychic in the Devil's Triangle*.

The calls that they took represented a cross-section of what the average American probably thinks about the question: Sure, there seems to be some kind of mystery, but how big a mystery? Plenty of airplanes and ships have gone down in the area, but how many incidents were due to bad weather? If there's a dangerous unknown energy there, why haven't scientists been able to identify it? Why doesn't the Government and its agencies own up to UFO sightings?

In other words, there is a sort of healthy skepticism that ordinary people, as opposed to those with vested interests, will usually take in a "fringe" subject: Maybe there's more in heaven and earth than meets the eye—but don't kid about inventing things to prove it. And in fact the incoming telephone call immediately before WFTL's equipment went on the blink was a typically sane one about whether, as reported, the local Coast Guard had actually spotted UFOs coming in and going out of the Bermuda Triangle. Ray Smithers replied that the area had a record of one of the highest concentrations of UFO sightings in the world, and it seemed likely that individual Coast Guardsmen were among those who had seen them. However, no report of this had been made official, just as there were similar rumors that other people working for Government or State authorities were sometimes reluctant to go on record about this sort of thing.

The calls were piling up—a logjam, it was later established, with dozens of subscribers getting the busy tone as they tried to get through to the studio. Ray Smithers decided to move on. "Let's go to another call." He pressed a connect button. "WFTL, you're on the air."

Nothing. Silence. He picked up another phone. "Well, there's no one on that line, let's try another. . . . Bermuda Triangle, you're on the air."

Again nothing. Ray Smithers was puzzled. "Uh, those lines are dead, let's try some more, let's see if we can get some calls on the air," he told listeners, pressing button after button, repeating again and again, "Bermuda Triangle, you're on the air."

As if he had suddenly been placed in a vacuum, nothing worked. WFTL's automatic switchboard to the nine studio lines was out of action to normal incoming calls—a freak phenomenon that has never happened before or since.

Then the silence was broken. One of the phones clicked into operation. The voice was deep, measured, somewhat distant, and seemed to have a curious knowing quality; whoever it was on the end of the line, according to Ray Smithers, he had an uncanny persistence. The message began:

"If there is one of you on the program who will understand what I'm going to say, it's that every living thing on this planet has an aura." Ray Smithers adjusted the level on the tape recorder. "The aura has its communications with the Millionth Counsel which governs this planet. The area that you are discussing now is the aura of this planet. It is the communicative channel through which the Millionth Counsel governs this planet."

Ray Smithers tried to interrupt: "Uh, which Counsel, sir?"

The voice continued with barely a hesitation. "Anyone going into the area, when the communicative channel is open, does not disappear. They are in the timeless void, and are all perfectly alive and well. It is the only area through which the Counsel can communicate with this planet. . . ."

There was a pause. Ray Smithers asked, "Are you there, sir?" No reply. Then, as suddenly as they had gone dead, the studio phones came back to life. Ray Smithers shrugged, picked up one of them, and carried on as if nothing had happened: "WFTL, Bermuda Triangle, you're on the air."

But evidently, something *had* happened—though just what, neither studio nor telephone engineers have ever been able to find out. A freak breakdown is one thing, a kooky phone call another; separately you might be inclined to pass them off, but when they happen together . . . ? Not only is the incident beyond coincidence, but conceivably it is part of a pattern of events that at last, perhaps, is beginning to reveal the secret of the Bermuda Triangle—a secret which currently seems beyond the grasp of scientists working even on the outermost fringes of scientific knowledge.

But it may be only just beyond. Even while the research team for the Warner Brothers film *Secrets of the Bermuda Triangle* was at work on what turned out to be the most wide-ranging investigation of the mystery yet undertaken, new scientific discoveries were being published in academic journals that threw new light on the mystery. Indeed, some people think an answer is so tantalizingly close that a new synthesis of this fringe science, a new way of looking at such relevant facts as are already known, could even now provide the basis for a solution.

To strive for this meant taking a fresh look at all the tragedies and oddities of the Triangle from three separate directions:

(1) Is there genuinely a mystery?

(2) Are any of the current explanations, orthodox or unorthodox, satisfactory on their own?

(3) What areas of scientific light can help unravel the oddest and least explicable incidents—for instance, the WFTL phone call?

In reference to the first question, it is clear that whatever critics in the various narrow branches of science may say, something strange is unquestionably happening in the Bermuda Triangle. The worldwide interest is itself phenomenal—as if the vast majority of people unconsciously "know" that there is something important to be discovered there.

This belief has persisted in spite of numerous attempts to explain all the disasters and disappearances in the Triangle (n.b., not just some, but *all*) as the result of a "natural" crisis—bad weather, malfunctioning of instruments, structural failure, human error, and so on. If this were a rational world, and people behaved as scientists expect them to, the Bermuda Triangle would long ago have ceased to exist even as a subject for barroom discussion.

But as everybody knows, it hasn't ceased to exist. And while scientists have been putting forward so-called rational explanations for all the strange examples of human and mechanical behavior in the Triangle, they have come up with the somewhat contradictory discovery that what happens in our minds (or brains) unwittingly has an effect on events outside. It is known, for instance, that the results of perfectly controlled experiments, untouched by human hand, are affected by the experimenter's belief in what is likely to take place. So, strange though it may seem, it is scientifically respectable to suggest that what people feel and believe about the Bermuda Triangle may influence what happens there, whether they themselves are in the Triangle or not.

How this happens is an unexplained oddity of quantum physics, and on this level, at least, it is therefore proved that there is without doubt a mystery surrounding the events of the Triangle: How much does unconscious human behavior play a part in the well-documented but unexplained happenings?

But you can also turn this question into reverse.

How much do unexplained and ill-understood changes in our surroundings affect what happens in our minds? What happens to us, for instance, if the barometric pressure drops, or there is a small change in the Earth's magnetic field? And here, as was documented more fully in later stages of the investigation, scientists have recently been coming up with discoveries that again do not in any way fit their comfortable existing theories. For the answer is that we are affected a great deal—once more, for reasons that are a total mystery.

So radical are these discoveries that the "straightforward" answer to all the deaths and disappearances of the Triangle can no longer be sensibly accepted without question. In Chapter Five is a summary of every major case mentioned by previous investigators, together with many new ones uncovered by the research team for the film. Treating each case conservatively, but in the light of the new scientific findings about the effects of man on his environment and vice versa, queries must be raised against the official explanation (or nonexplanation) in no less than 70 out of the 147 cases. (The number of cases itself is improbably large.)

It remains true, of course, that in the majority of cases the orthodox explanations of bad weather, or of some form of structural or mechanical defect, hold good. But even here, we now have to ask other, more basic, questions. Why was there structural or mechanical (or electrical) failure in seaworthy ships and flight-tested planes? Was it some man-machine interaction? Or was it some as yet undiscovered, perhaps extraterrestrial force, the same one that may be the reason for the absence of wreckage in so many cases?

The answer is that we just don't know for certain —yet. But it has always seemed too sweeping to gather up every mysterious disappearance in the Triangle and put each one in a wastebasket marked "natural causes." These new discoveries on the outskirts of science only confirm what more skeptical observers have always felt: You have to look elsewhere for the answer. So a mystery exists, even in scientific terms, and this brings us to the second line of inquiry—how much can we be helped by the unorthodox explanations that have already been proposed?

No less than seventeen of these explanations have now been suggested. In alphabetical rank, rather than order of probability, they are:

1. ALIEN KIDNAPPING. Specimen-hungry residents from outer space (or another dimension, or from a base beneath the ocean) scoop up ships and planes and their inhabitants for research and observation.

2. ANTI-GRAVITATION/ANTIMATTER. Developments in particle physics, said to be largely secret and unpublished, indicate that forces are known which can cause solid objects to disappear, either by being placed in an excessively large magnetic field, or when contact is made with certain antigravitational particles of a nature completely contrary to those that make up our known universe.

3. ATLANTIS ENERGY. The "sleeping prophet" Edgar Cayce psychically divined that ancient Atlanteans used crystals as a power source, anticipating the 20th-century discovery of the laser beam; some of these still exist near Bimini and are occasionally activated with disastrous consequences.

4. CATASTROPHIC WEATHER. Weather phenomena sometimes occur that are on a different scale from those predicted and measured by meteorological bureaus, often associated with falling objects from the sky (ice blocks, meteorites); it is not known what triggers these, but their severity, it is said, would be enough to account for all but the largest of disappearing ships.

5. CLEAR AIR TURBULENCE. The aerial counterparts of tidal waves are the results of collisions of opposing winds. It can happen vertically or horizontally, and the effect on light aircraft is conceivably disastrous, tearing them apart and cutting off their radio communications simultaneously.

6. COMPASS VARIATIONS. It so happens that the Bermuda Triangle and the "Devil's Sea" south of Japan are in areas where magnetic north and true north coincide; this is said to create navigational difficulties and wildly spinning compasses.

7. COSMIC BOMBARDMENT. The Earth is normally protected from harmful cosmic rays, and from the high-powered "solar wind" emanating from the sun, by the Van Allen belts in space (a product of the Earth's magnetic field). If this were briefly penetrated, cosmic bombardment could disintegrate ships and planes and annihilate life.

8. GIANT FIREBALLS. Ball lightning is now an observed and accepted scientific fact, although its nature is not understood. Sufficiently large ones, striking at random, could be enough to destroy anything carrying quantities of hydrocarbons, i.e., fuel tanks in planes and ships.

9. MAELSTROMS/WHIRLPOOLS. The Sargasso Sea, a significant part of the Triangle, consists

of slow-moving currents that form a giant whirl-pool; perhaps freak conditions sometimes occur so that the center of this becomes the maelstrom long enshrined in seafaring legend, where the victims are said to sail through "the depths of the sea" to the "lowest bowels of the earth."

10. MAGNETIC EARTHQUAKES. The nature of the Earth's magnetic field, which alters all the time, is not well understood scientifically; however, it has been suggested that we are coming toward a magnetic crisis of some kind, and telltale signs of this can be seen in underwater earthquake conditions in the Triangle.

11. MAGNETIC STORMS. The bad weather which accompanies many of the tragedies may have a more subtle effect than was thought, in the way that the associated magnetic changes can un-hinge the human mind and at the same time cause optical and mechanical illusions.

12. OCEAN-BED INSTABILITY. The theory of continental drift is now an accepted scientific fact —huge plates of land known as the lithosphere gradually move away from and toward each other. At the edges, where they meet, mountains form and chasms appear; the resulting ocean disturbance would be enough to swallow up small craft.

13. REVERSED VORTEXES/NEGATIVE PYR-AMIDS. These two theories can be linked, since their effects are similar—boats, ships, and people are thrown forcibly into outer space. Causes suggested are (i) an ascending whirlpool of air; (ii) two pyramids placed apex to apex beneath the sea, producing "negative" energy (the opposite of normal pyramid energy).

14. SEA MONSTERS. Stories of squids fighting titanic battles with whales are cited in support of the possibility that monsters from the deep could be responsible for at least some of the missing small boats.

15. SPACE-TIME ABERRATIONS. Involving the notion of another dimension, these aberrations are perhaps associated with the theory of black holes, into which the disappearing ships and planes somehow slip.

16. TIDAL WAVES. Freak waves, some even 200 feet high, are known to exist; they can be caused by underwater seismic disturbances—earthquakes, volcanoes, landslides, continental drift—of a sort thought to be prevalent in the area of the Bermuda Triangle.

17. WATERSPOUTS. Generally these are whirling columns of air picking up a light sea spray, but under storm conditions they may theoretically turn into seagoing tornadoes. If the conditions are right, a waterspout could stretch from the surface of the ocean up to the clouds above.

So there is almost an embarrassment of alternative theories to choose from, and perhaps the most immediately noticeable thing about them is that not one seems at first glance comprehensive—none of them can explain *all* the disappearances. Indeed, as the film investigation proceeded, this was, quite properly, confirmed. It would be just as wrong to try to ascribe every disaster to one alternative theory as it is to ascribe them all to a single natural cause. What happens in the Bermuda Triangle is complicated, and it is only to be expected that many of the theories have common elements and overlap.

However, the challenge of trying to find some unifying element, some overall pattern in the underlying causes, remains. To begin with, on what criteria should a serious investigation be based?

First, only to accept evidence that has been well proved or demonstrated. This means raising a skeptical eyebrow at a number of the theories above, for unless there is some kind of a scientific or historical basis for us to look at, we are dealing with "invented" theories that can never, by their nature, be proved.

This means discarding, or at least regarding as insignificant in the broad picture, theory 14, since the largest octopus ever caught had a diameter little more than 20 feet, and although the eel is said to grow to 45 feet, even this extreme estimate by oceanographers can hardly produce catastrophic effects on large ships. Theory 9 also goes by the board, since none of these giant whirlpools have ever been observed in the area; those in the Sargasso Sea are tame by comparison with their Norwegian counterparts. Theory 1 also goes out: quite apart from the inherent unlikelihood of extraterrestrials picking on outdated planes and undistinguished small boats, there is no direct evidence whatsoever for it—it is an *ad hoc* theory brought forward quite unnecessarily in the light of the wealth of alternative explanations readily available.

Purists might also say that a number of other theories should also be discarded for lack of observable evidence, notably 3 and 13, which depend on so far undiscovered underwater forms of ancient energy; 6, because there is no good reason why a compass pointing due north should cause any navigational difficulty; and 10, since a magnetic earthquake has never been scientifically recorded. However, although all these criticisms are true, it may be too soon to dismiss the theories *in toto*. Parts of what is suggested are certainly lacking in proof, but there are nevertheless elements of originality and insight that enable them to be considered under the next criterion for the investigation, which is:

Second, be open-minded about accepting unlikely facts, even if at first they do not seem to fit. Scientific advances are invariably made through unlikely connections between hitherto unlinked ideas; nor should the power of coincidence be denied, for this too has an "other-dimensional" aspect that may be of help in unlocking the secret of the Triangle.

Third, accept that any explanation finally arrived at must resolve why the phenomena that occur in the Triangle seem to be selective: One plane may disappear while another only a few miles away remains safe; similarly with boats. For this reason theory 7 can be firmly discarded. It is in any case poorly based in science, since the protective shield of the Van Allen belts has never been observed to vary significantly in intensity, and it is constantly monitored by satellites. But even under the supposed freak conditions when this may have happened, the havoc that would be wrought on Earth generally, let alone in the Bermuda Triangle, would be universally catastrophic.

In the case of what happened on WFTL, applying the three criteria meant first of all trying to establish the truth of what happened there. As far as the electronic breakdown was concerned, nobody has been inclined to offer a realistic explanation; similar sorts of events happen occasionally in radio and TV stations the world over because of faulty fuses, overheating, frequency overloading, and so on—but never in *exactly* the way that it happened to Ray Smithers that evening (so far as is known), where it first looked as if the main input had been unplugged (it hadn't), but left a parallel circuit free to carry the mystery voice and message. So for the moment it remains an inexplicable fact.

As for the message, a tape of it was taken to John Hickman of Los Angeles, a certified voice stress analyst. By an electronic study of stress variations of the electromagnetic patterns recorded on a strip chart, he is able to tell what parts of a particular speech are of special importance to the person, and whether the person is being truthful or not. In the WFTL recording brought to him, he had no doubt that two of the sentences quoted ("They do not disappear, they are in the timeless void. . . ." and "It is the only area through which the Counsel can communicate. . . .") were the most significant. John Hickman concluded his report: "The patterns exhibited on the strip chart indicate that this was not a prank or a hoax call, and the caller believes what he is saying."

So, as far as has been possible, the authenticity of both the phone breakdown and the message is now established. But the incident has another aspect—perhaps the first of those revealing connections and coincidences which occurred during the investigation, for the message led quickly to what turned out to be the true story of Flight 19. This, the most renowned and best-documented of Triangle disappearances, in which six U.S. Navy planes vanished without trace in 1945, is surely one which demands an unorthodox explanation, for it contains unmistakable signs of man-machine madness. The incident also, as we shall see, contains that other-dimensional element which is so frustrating to a scientific observer, since it is so difficult to record. Yet maddening and unprovable though it may be, this aspect—call it psychic, supernatural, or what you will—is so much a part of the continuing theme of the Triangle mystery that a thorough investigation cannot afford to ignore it— indeed, cannot avoid it. In WFTL, the way it emerged was like this:

In the studio, the psychic Page Bryant had remained silent during the strange telephone call. Ray Smithers had been concerned to see her face collapse a little, as if in sorrow, and a small tear run down her cheek. Afterwards, he asked her sympathetically what she had been thinking about. Her reply (which she later repeated to researchers) was that the message had put her in touch with one of the dead aircraftmen. In interpreting this, we should remember that time and again she has been shown to be highly gifted psychically, by all accounts able to be dramatically accurate about past and present events and to some extent also able to foresee the future. In December 1974, for instance, she was on a live radio show when, some minutes *before* it happened, she spontaneously started to describe the location and circumstances of the appalling plane crash at Jacksonville, Florida.

Like many other psychics, Page Bryant is perfectly certain that there is a strange power, or energy source, connected with the Triangle, which she can sense and at the same time use in order to tune in to what is happening there. Probably the first well-known psychic to visit the area with the aim of recording her experiences and her insight (in 1969), she has now been there more than a dozen times and is a friend of many of the major investigators of the phenomena. On the first occasion, she chartered a plane to fly out from Miami eastward, and describes what happened as "the most incredible experience, the most dramatic psychic experience, that I've ever had."

She says that on that day, as in the WFTL studio, she came vividly in touch with the dying moments of Air Sergeant Robert Francis Gallivan at the time when his plane spun out of control and vanished—"more realistic than the most terrifying dream, so close you felt you could touch what was going on." But try as she did, she was unable on that first occasion to tune into the exact cause of what made him go out of control—"and that's the reason why I made so many trips back over the area afterwards: I wanted to know." Today, she maintains that Gallivan and all the other fliers are dead—in her words, "they've gone into the dimension of what we call dead. There's magnetic energy in that Triangle area; I know because I've experienced it, and I'm calling it magnetic because I don't know anything else to call it. It's some kind of a vortex, and it has an effect on the mind as well as the body, a psychological effect which causes disorientation. That's what happened to the leader on Flight 19 in the first place, why he started going adrift in clear weather, I'm sure of it."

In common with other psychics, Page Bryant admits that it is extremely difficult to put into our normal day-to-day language many of the insights which she obtains psychically. But however imprecise her description of what caused the disappearance of Flight 19, it is strikingly similar to what is now shown to be scientifically possible. It is also consistent with the behavior of the pilots, the confusion of the ground staff, and with a new piece of testimony concerning what happened: the experience of aircraftman Eagle Bolotin, the man who escaped from Flight 19.

Ever since the mystery of the Triangle first came under scrutiny, the events surrounding the disappearance of Flight 19 have been subjected to minute investigation. The Navy's own inquiry took several months, and the subsequent report was more than 400 pages long. Inevitably, some recollections of what happened have become blurred with time; equally, what people say to official inquiries may be only part of the truth, since they are bound to answer within the framework of the question that was put to them.

The research team for *Secrets of the Bermuda Triangle* went back over all the printed evidence and, where possible, interviewed those people present at Fort Lauderdale on the fateful day when the flight of Avengers and the Master Mariner rescue aircraft took off. What emerges from this unwritten and often unrevealed evidence is a pattern of events entirely consistent with the suggestion that experienced people sometimes become inexplicably disoriented when they fly over the Triangle; and that this "other dimension" talked about by psychics is felt unwittingly by people who would not normally suppose them to be receptive to it.

Eagle Bolotin first.

Eagle Bolotin was the pilot who got away. As he puts it now: "I had the feeling that a big hand had taken hold and saved me. I realize how that sounds—at least I can guess how that sounds—but these are my most inner feelings." The way it happened was that, as a matter of habit, he regularly volunteered to fly under other people's names. "I loved flying, some of the other guys didn't, so I used their names to help them get in the number of flight hours needed on the record so they could qualify for extra pay. That afternoon in December, I went out after lunch to fly again in the afternoon. As luck would have it, and that's certainly the word, the Duty Officer was the same man who had been there in the morning when I had already flown."

So the Duty Officer threw him off the flight, and Eagle Bolotin has lived to be able to tell the tale today. But that first piece of luck, or coincidence, was followed by another, and yet another. The Duty Officer, Allen Kosnar, then became inexplicably worried himself, and took himself off the flight (as he was entitled to do, because of the number of hours he had already flown). "To this day, I can't explain the strange reason that made me do it," he says now.

And then a third flyer had qualms—the Flight Leader, Lieutenant Charles C. Taylor, a six-year flying veteran with more than 2,500 hours in the air. A newcomer to Fort Lauderdale, he was unaccountably and uncharacteristically 30 minutes late for the briefing, something which colleagues who knew him as a punctual and conscientious pilot had not known happen before. The reason, witnesses from the air base now recall, was that he was shut in a room with a handful of fellow officers trying to rationalize his instinctive unease that something—he didn't know what—was wrong. But he couldn't pinpoint it, so in the end he shrugged his shoulders and marched into the briefing room with a brief apology to the men.

We can see now that those first intangible premonitions fit into a spiral of increasing confusion that only ended some four and a half hours later with the final breakdown of radio communication and the loss of all five Avenger planes on the flight, together with Charles Taylor and the entire crew of thirteen. Going back over the evidence, it is clear that the basic facts are true as reported: The planes were in good condition, and fully equipped; the radios began to function strangely; the men suffered a gross form of disorientation whose cause has not been properly established.

Avenger planes, even from this distance in time, were machines to be proud of. Powered by a 1600 horsepower Wright Cyclone engine, they could fly at nearly 300 mph and carry 2,000 pounds of bombs or a torpedo. On this day, they were carrying enough fuel to give them a range of 1,000 miles. They were well made to withstand the occasional disaster, such as an over-run on an aircraft carrier's flight deck, for in addition to a design capability for making smooth water landings, they could stay afloat in any water for 90 seconds. The crews, for this reason, had been trained to make an emergency exit in 60 seconds. At the same time, access to the life rafts was from outside the plane. On an uncounted number of earlier occasions Navy Rescue craft had rescued survivors, wet and cold but otherwise unharmed, from the kind of crash landing which the "natural causes" explanation supposes happened to Flight 19.

So something else seems to have been happening apart from straightforward mechanical or operational malfunctioning. It was, after all, a normal, somewhat boring, training flight of the kind that all the men concerned had taken part in many times before. Eagle Bolotin remembers what they were like:

"Our business used to be to fly a triangular course. On the way out we would sometimes drop a dummy torpedo under an old World War I destroyer. From the air you could see the bubble line, and the torpedo was set deep so that it would actually go under the old vessel, and we could see whether it would have been a hit or a miss. But the main purpose of the hop was navigational experience—not difficult when you'd put in the number of flying hours that we had, just routine in fact."

A similar flight exercise had taken place in the morning, and when Charles Taylor took off with his five Avengers in the afternoon there was, to start with, little untoward. The torpedo run went off as scheduled, and at 3 p.m., according to several sources, they were seen by a fisherman on the first leg of their triangular flight, dead on course.

That was the last time they were seen. From now on, what happened has to be extracted from the increasingly bizarre radio messages that were reported to the official Navy investigation and recalled subsequently by participants.

PHASE ONE began at 3:40, by which time the flight should have been about to turn into the northward leg of its northward run, and Taylor was out of direct radio contact with headquarters at Fort Lauderdale. However, the senior instructor from the air base there, Lieutenant Robert Cox, had just taken off on another mission, and for the next 45 critical minutes he was able to listen and talk to the flight—the crews' only contact with the outside world.

The first disturbing snatch of conversation which Cox (call sign FT-74) picked up was Charles Taylor (call sign FT-28) talking to another pilot, Marine Captain Edward Powers.

Taylor: Powers, what does your compass read? (Pause.)
Repeat to Powers, what does your compass read?
I don't know where we are.
I'm afraid we got lost after that last turn.

Cox reported back to Fort Lauderdale what he had just heard—"Somebody up here, some boats or planes seem to be lost"—and then tried to contact the flight.

Cox: This is FT-74 to boats or planes calling Powers. Please identify yourselves so we can send some help.
Taylor: Uh, this is FT-28. Does anyone have any suggestions?
Cox: FT-28, this is FT-74, what is the problem?
Taylor: Both of my compasses are out. I am trying to find Fort Lauderdale, Florida. I am over land, but it is broken. I am sure it's the Keys, but I have no idea how far out I am.

From ground control, Cox received instructions. He passed them on.

Cox: FT-28, this is FT-74. Put the sun on your port wing and if you're in the Keys, fly up the coast. What is your present altitude? I'll fly to meet you.

By now, there were beginning to be signs that something other than compass failure might be involved. Taylor was beginning to stammer, and his speech was becoming a little slurred. What he said was not quite rational.

> *Taylor:* I—I know where I am now. I'm at twenty-three hundred feet. Don't come after me. . . . Can you have Miami or someone turn on their radar gear and pick us up? We are on a navigational hop and on the second leg. I took over as I thought we were lost. Unfortunately, both of my compasses are not working. Over.

Noticing the contradictions in what Taylor was saying ("I know where I am," "Can someone . . . pick us up"), Cox tried to persuade him to switch on his emergency IFF gear (which would have increased the chance of his plane's being picked up on somebody's radar) and his ZBX gear (a homing device). His reply from Taylor was "negative"—either the devices wouldn't work, or Taylor wouldn't switch them on; either way, the result was the same. Taylor was becoming increasingly isolated and confused. Ground control, concerned at the situation, instructed Cox to make Taylor hand over control to another pilot. Cox tried.

> *Cox:* FT-28, this is FT-74. Have one of your wingmen take over the lead. FT-28, your transmission is fading. Something seems to be wrong. What is your present altitude?
> *Taylor:* (sound fading): I'm at forty-five hundred feet, visibility ten to twelve miles. . . .

By now it was 4:20. Taylor was reporting inconsistencies about his equipment and his height. As if whatever was happening was infectious, Cox's own radio abruptly ceased to function. Phase One was drawing to an end with the weather bright and clear, the sun going down in the west—a simple navigational point for a schoolboy, let alone a flier of Taylor's experience. The wind was around 30 knots—enough to whip up white caps on the sea beneath, but negligible in terms of the Avengers' 300 mph top speed.

Cox came in to land, and (wrongly, it seems in retrospect) was refused permission to go on back-up mission in another plane. To this day, it ranks as one of the most frustrating experiences in his life. As to what went wrong, he still doesn't know: "The leader of Flight 19 admitted that he was lost. He at no time admitted that he had any other difficulties, except that he believed that his compasses didn't work properly. For some forty-five minutes I gave him assistance by radio. He either refused or ignored the help that was being given him."

PHASE TWO continued to be marked by poor and intermittent radio communication, this time from the ground station of Port Everglades, which was able, however unsatisfactorily, to take up where Cox had left off. During the next hour and a half, acting in concert with other bases that occasionally were able to establish a radio "fix" on the doomed flight, they established (a) that Lieutenant Taylor had never been lost in the first place, and (b) that if he and the rest of the Avengers had followed navigational instructions issued from Port Everglades, they would have arrived back safely.

But it was too late. As one observer at the time now puts it: "Something up there was terribly wrong. The compasses had gone, a man's mind had gone. . . ." The snatches of dialogue between

Taylor and the ground show he was hopelessly confused.

> *Controller:* Port Everglades to FT-28, radio check. Can you read us?
> *Taylor:* Affirmative. We have just passed over a small island. There is no other land in sight. I'm at thirty-five hundred feet [after reporting 4,500 feet a few moments earlier]. Have on emergency IFF. Does anyone in the area have a radar screen that could pick us up?
> *Controller:* Roger. Suggest you have another good plane in your flight with a good compass take over the lead and guide you back to the airport.
> *Taylor:* Roger.

Taylor may or may not have understood the message. There seemed to be a garbled conversation between the various pilots. However, a few minutes later he was still leading the flight, and continued to do so in spite of the fact that he was by now changing direction meaninglessly. He even refused to alter radio frequencies to obtain better communication with the ground.

> *Controller:* Port Everglades to FT-28. If you can change to yellow band, 3,000 kilocycle emergency frequency, please do so and give us a call.
> *Taylor:* I cannot switch frequencies. I must keep my planes intact.

At various times the ground stations heard, desperately aware of their futility to do anything to affect the situation, Taylor's zigzag navigational instructions to the rest of the flight.

Taylor: One of the planes thinks if we went 270 degrees we would hit land. . . .

Taylor: We are heading 030 degrees for 45 minutes, then we will fly north to make sure we are not over the Gulf of Mexico. . . .

Taylor: Change course to 090 degrees for ten minutes. . . .

Taylor: We are now flying 270 degrees. We will fly 270 degrees until we hit the beach or run out of gas. Okay, when the first man gets down to ten gallons of gas, we will all go down together. Does everybody understand that?

These were almost the last words Taylor was heard to utter. A last, despairing attempt was made to persuade him to switch radio frequencies. Then, ironically, at almost exactly the moment when ground control was at last able to pinpoint the flight's position north of the Bahamas and east of Florida, radio communication finally ceased.

Neither the mystery nor the tragedy ended there, for a Mariner flying boat, with thirteen aboard, was instantly dispatched to the exact place on the map where the Avengers had at last been located. On its way this plane also vanished, probably from an explosion—its sort were known as "flying gas tanks," notoriously subject to explosions should there be a chance spark or an illegally lit cigarette. So its disappearance is perhaps not so much of a mystery as it has been made out to be; maybe a verdict of "natural causes" is reasonable in this case.

Except for one thing, about which Eagle Bolotin is emphatic even now.

The lack of wreckage.

"There's nothing to explain why we didn't find

any remains. There were hundreds of planes went out at first light the next morning to look for the Avengers and the Mariner, including mine, and when you do one of those searches, whether it's a spiral search or a square search, it's the same thing, you don't miss much. The shelf round there is shallow for a long way out, and you can see things from the air that tell you when there's been a crash or a sinking. Five, six planes—there should have been something floating around, a Mae West, some sailor's cap, you know...."

As for why the Avengers lost their way, Eagle Bolotin is equally mystified. "When people ask me what I think happened to those people, I don't have any fancy answers. I'll tell you what I think happened, and it's just an educated guess. I think they became disoriented, didn't know where they were going or in what direction, and that's kind of hard to explain. But you know, I keep hearing stories about the magnetic compass needle spinning...."

Finally there is the third mystery in the loss of Flight 19—the intangible one, the stroke of fortune that kept Eagle Bolotin off the flight, the premonitions of Allen Kosnar and Charles Taylor. The investigation showed that this sort of thing is far from uncommon in the Triangle. More than twenty years later, on January 11, 1967, a photographer named Oscar Barber felt exactly the same way—and coincidentally in the same place—now renamed Fort Lauderdale International Airport—that it happened to the three men who missed Flight 19. After helping to load motion picture gear onto a converted Chase YC-122 cargo plane, he decided to miss the trip and go by scheduled airline instead.

To this day, he has no explanation. The Chase YC-122 was not overloaded—indeed, as a large glider converted to a propeller aircraft with the addition of two engines, it was theoretically supposed to have added stability. But as Oscar Barber seems to have unconsciously predicted, it crashed without a known reason some thirty miles northwest of Bimini. Asked the reason for his absence, Barber simply says, "I just had a feeling that I should go by commercial airline."

Within a week, a further two aircraft went missing: a Beechcraft Bonanza from Miami International Airport, and a Piper Apache on a flight from San Juan to St. Thomas. Their flight plan was known in detail, their last known position almost exactly. Yet in spite of the usual thorough and extensive search, no wreckage was found. Another coincidence? Or set of coincidences?

The triple mystery of solid objects disappearing, of human minds disintegrating, and of other-dimensional coincidences forcing themselves upon the scene became the principal continuing puzzle within the investigation. Later on, it became apparent that there was a feasible way in which they might be linked. But now it was time to go back to basics in the true scientific sense: to find out what is known about the fundamental forces that are thought to govern our observable universe, and to see which of these might conceivably apply to the challenge presented by events in the Bermuda Triangle.

It soon became clear that there was only one candidate.

The myriad wavelengths of electromagnetism.

CHAPTER TWO

Magnets of Life

In the Middle East, Jews and Arabs alike have a common enemy: the searing, enervating wind known as the khamsin or sharav, which burns its way out of the desert each spring and autumn, for approximately 150 days out of the year. It blows up from Africa and sweeps across the Sinai Peninsula, picking up hot air and dust and bringing in a variety of unpleasant effects along with it.

Everyone there knows what it's like when it's happening. The dry air makes your feet swell painfully, your eyes and nose itch; if you are an asthma sufferer, the chances are you will soon be gasping for breath. So when people are able to, they retreat inside and practice the oriental virtues of patience and forbearance.

These symptoms have been known throughout history. But until the 1960s nobody realized that this wind had another effect—an effect so unusual that it took some years for any of the scientific journals to be convinced that what was reported was real.

People know, and animals know, that the wind is on its way long in advance of its actual arrival.

They can't feel its force physically against their skin, because the air may be as still as a stagnant drain. They can't feel a change of temperature—it hasn't happened yet. If they are noticing the beginnings of a change in barometric pressure, no scientist can explain the bodily mechanism that allows this to happen.

And that's what all the fuss is about. According to the rule book, there is no way in which we ought to be able to detect the approach of the khamsin, or other winds like it—the sirocco in Italy, the foehn in southern Europe, the mistral in France, or the chinook and the Santa Ana winds in North America. There is so much molecular activity in our bodies that the energy generated ought to swamp the tiny electromagnetic changes that herald the wind's arrival—so tiny, indeed, that they are measurable only with the most sophisticated laboratory equipment.

But somehow this doesn't happen. It seems we unconsciously detect and process these signals, and our minds react to them accordingly. We "know" that a change in the weather is on the way.

The relevance for an investigation of the Triangle mystery is this: At the same time as we instinctively sense that this subtle change in our environment is taking place, some people's behavior is drastically affected. Admissions to mental hospitals rise markedly. The imminent arrival of the khamsin drives a few incurably insane. The suicide rate goes up. There are more violent and irrational crimes, and more automobile accidents. Young people become tense, irritable, and occasionally lash out physically; older people become fatigued, apathetic, depressed, and sometimes faint.

The approach of the khamsin is not alone in producing these strange psychological effects. Dr. Robert O. Becker, at the Veterans Administration Hospital in Syracuse, New York, has established conclusively that thunderstorms, and the associated changes in magnetic field intensity, create disturbed behavior in mental patients. As with the approach of the khamsin, there are more suicides, more cases of violence and irrationality.

In other words, it is now known that there is a direct link between the weather and disordered mental conditions, and so far as the Triangle is concerned, it is surprising that other investigations have not noticed this somewhat obvious connection. There is, after all, an immediate similarity between the behavior of Charles Taylor in Flight 19 and many of the symptoms described above.

However, the subject in question—the biological effects of low-level electric and magnetic fields—is not a simple or straightforward one, and for many years it was shunned by the scientific establishment. Robert Becker himself says that since he began his work "the response to our reports has changed from complete rejection through amused disbelief to—at present—enthusiastic acceptance." Even now, the hunt for what has been discovered takes an investigator to many strange and obscure scientific journals which do not always have the space to print all the evidence that is accumulating. Dr. Becker's optimism notwithstanding, it is difficult to avoid the conclusion that the weight of orthodox scientific opinion would prefer to ignore or reject the evidence, in much the way that it takes the same attitude toward the Bermuda Triangle itself.

The central problem is that the idea of people being affected by minute electromagnetic changes is very difficult to fit into the scheme of knowledge that has been prepared for us. Electromagnetic waves, except in the narrow part of the spectrum that we perceive as light and color—our visual image of the world around us—are invisible. A little more of the spectrum beneath this narrow band can be felt as heat. Above the visible band are all the frequencies that, even if we can't feel them, are well understood by scientists because of their danger to human life—the X-rays, gamma rays, and cosmic rays that in sufficient quantity cause mutation and death.

That still leaves a vast, almost infinite number of wavelengths deep in the electromagnetic spectrum that supposedly have no effect on us whatsoever. The trouble is, as we have seen above, that they do.

From February 18 to 24, 1973, in Aspen, Colorado, an important conference on the subject was held, attended by 115 scientists from Canada, France, Germany, Japan, and the United States, the vast majority of them frustrated and dissatisfied with the low priority being given to the subject by their respective Governments. In a long opening address that ranged widely over the new discoveries being made, James B. Beal of the World Institute in New York, said a great deal that may be of relevance to the Triangle mystery.

Consider, for instance, how the known instability of the seabed in the Triangle area may give rise to some of the effects he described in this passage:

There are several interesting electromagnetic field effects associated with earthquakes, also electrostatic and ionic. An earthquake causes a build-up in pressure in surrounding rocks; if these rocks are predominantly crystalline in nature the piezoelectric effect is present and tremendous amounts of energy are stored up, which may be occasionally released just before an earthquake, as in Japan where "earthquake lightning" can occur in a cloudless sky or in Tashkent in 1966 when a "sky glow" preceded the quake by several hours. The earthquake produces a sudden, drastic change in the earth's magnetic and electric field. This local field change is of a characteristic signature pattern and propagates at the speed of light, while the earthquake travels at about the speed of sound, or slower; hence animals sense a sudden change in the usually stable, slowly changing environmental background low-frequency and electrostatic fields. This is unusual, so the animal is alerted, nervous, and prepared for danger.

There is no need to be put off by the somewhat technical language that he uses, for the message is clear. Animals can sense when an earthquake is about to happen, and their behavior changes; presumably the same thing happens with humans. And both the "lightning" and the crystalline effects that he cites are strongly reminiscent of those "solutions" to the Triangle mystery which invoke UFOs, or the supposed power source of ancient Atlanteans.

At a later stage in his address, James Beal asserted in a memorable phrase, "As a product of the cosmos, we are all tuned in." In other words, whether we like it or not, we are all liable to be affected by unknown cosmic influences somewhere in the range of electromagnetic radiation. Most of the time, we manage to keep our balance, even under effects of such conditions as the khamsin; but some of us, sometimes, can become unhinged.

Remembering that at this stage we are dealing with only one of the three aspects of the Triangle mystery, disorientation, (i.e., not disappearance of solid bodies, nor—yet—the appearance of other-dimensional phenomena), we can see how many of the classic cases in Triangle literature are related to these new scientific discoveries. The confusion and uncertainty surrounding the events of Flight 19 are examples that have already been quoted; the almost equally notorious last voyage of the USS *Cyclops*, and the steadily deteriorating mental state of its captain, George Worley, can now also be seen in a fresh light.

Although the event happened so long ago—during the winter of 1917/18—a surprising amount of accurate information about the case turns out to be available. The following reconstruction has been put together from a variety of sources: personal eyewitness accounts, the Maritime Registry, U.S. Weather Bureau reports, and the official records of the U.S. Navy. The basic fact to emerge is that, after all this time, there is still no satisfactory explanation for why such a large, relatively new (only seven years old) ship, the first to be equipped with radio, should vanish without trace and without sending an SOS message. It is still an unsolved Triangle mystery.

Moreover, during our investigation, it became clear that Worley grew increasingly irrational as he moved from the crisp northern climate of Norfolk, Virginia, where the harbor was frozen and liberty parties from ships at anchor walked on the ice, to the sultry heat of the tropics, where, as we shall see, Worley had become so deranged as to carry out barefooted punishment drill on the burning decks.

At the beginning of the voyage, there is some evidence that Commander George Worley knew he was unwell, or on the brink of being so, but was still able to deal with the matter in a rational way. He sold some property in Norfolk, including the home where he lived his shore life contentedly with his wife and child, so that on returning from his fateful voyage he could have an operation for an unidentified illness and then spend at least six months in California recuperating. A photograph was taken of him just before he left, standing—a first hint of doom?—with his little girl on one of the *Cyclops*'s life preservers. His last words to her were: "Here, give your old dad a big hug—one that'll last all the way from Norfolk to Rio and back home again." Then he kissed his wife fondly and his family left the ship; nothing here to hint of the disordered behavior that was to come.

Many men, of course, have two personalities—one for home and one for work—and George Worley was no exception. Conrad A. Nervig, a newly appointed ensign on the voyage south to Rio de Janeiro, said many years later that although he was personally well treated by Worley, this was an exception. As a rule he was "unfriendly and taciturn, generally disliked by both his officers and his men . . . the kind of gruff eccentric salt of the

41

old school who considered their crews not as human beings but only as a means of getting their vessels to the next port."

As this was his first voyage under Worley's command, Conrad Nervig has no way of comparing the atmosphere with that of previous trips; in the wardroom, it seemed to become progressively gloomier as the ship moved south. "It was such a depressing place because of his behavior. Everyone was unhappy. Worley began to pick on people for imagined wrongs." It got so bad with one young officer, Ensign Cain, that the ship's doctor became convinced he was going to commit suicide and had him placed in the ship's sick bay just to get him out of the way of Worley.

That incident happened on the fifth day out when the ship, in damp and warm weather, was in the vicinity of the Bermuda Triangle. On the same day, after a trivial disagreement, Worley placed his executive officer Lieutenant Forbes under arrest in the confinement of his cabin—the first time such a thing had happened. From now on he became increasingly irrational. Had some unrecorded climatic change in the Triangle affected his mind? He took to rising in the middle of the night and taking nocturnal walks around his ship, carrying the cane that was always in his hand and wearing nothing but long woollen underwear and a derby hat.

On these occasions his other, more pleasant, personality came to life; he told Ensign Nervig long, unconnected, mostly humorous anecdotes about his life at sea. He had a fund of such stories, and they would pour out of him like an old man's ramblings, almost insane, oblivious to interruptions or what was happening to his ship—even on one occasion carrying on in spite of the pandemonium that occurred when a hatch blew off one of the ship's turbines. Next morning, he refused to let it be mended, and when it was pointed out that to sail on the one remaining engine was putting unnecessary strain on it, he replied simply (but prophetically), "She'll last as long as we do."

These symptoms of schizophrenia, of a refusal to face reality, are well known nowadays to psychiatrists, although in those days it would simply have been marked down to obstinacy. Similarly his disciplinary actions, then regarded only as severe, would today be marked down as dangerously sadistic.

They reached their height in Rio, at the end of January 1918, when the *Cyclops* had finally reached the limit of its southern journey (and the weather, perhaps significantly, was hotter than at any other time). The atmosphere on the ship, already doom-laden, became even more macabre with the arrival of five prisoners convicted the previous month for crimes ranging from murder to being AWOL. Worley was ordered to take them back to the United States on his homeward leg; so rumor-filled was his ship that many believed the murderer, Fireman First Class James Coker, was to be executed during the journey.

Whether or not this happened has never been established. But impeccable accounts tell of Worley conducting punishment drills with the five manacled prisoners and other members of the crew accused of minor breaches of the ship's rules. A .45 automatic in his hand, he would command the men to bare their feet, and then to walk a "dead" march in slow motion around the sunlit deck, the unbearably hot iron burning into their soles, sweat dripping from their faces. At the end of the march they would be forced to stand to attention in the sun, for as long as he thought fit. Worley then ordered "at ease" and "attention," often waiting until a number of men had passed out before stopping. Only then did he allow cold water to be hosed onto the men's feet. Reports say the decks were so hot that when it hit the deck, it hissed. Not for nothing was the *Cyclops* called "the hell ship."

Before the *Cyclops* set off homeward, there was another incident that seemed to many people to symbolize the chaos deriving from Worley's now obvious instability. As the ship took on her last major load of cargo—coal, manganese, heavy packing cases—a motor-power sail ship was maneuvering under sail near the stern when, inadvertently, her motor was switched on and she made a lunge forward. A seaman who had been leaning over the rail trying to make a rope fast was hauled over the edge. In the water, screaming, he was sucked into the vortex of water created by the *Cyclops*'s propeller and died horribly.

Conrad Nervig left the *Cyclops* at Rio, and from this point onward the narrative has to be pieced together from second-hand information; none of the people remaining on the ship lived to tell the tale. But there are some significant pieces of evidence showing that whatever had happened to Worley's mind was now irrevocable—no compensating improvement set in on the northbound voyage that should have ended back in the relative cool of Baltimore. Nervig himself made contact once more, from the ship to which he had been transferred, when he took mail aboard the *Cyclops*. His diary noted that *Cyclops* "stood in from the north," the opposite direction from the one that Worley should have been navigating. Clearly, things were still wrong. The weather, for the record, was typical for the season in Brazil: The heat wave had been broken by the arrival of the midsummer rains, and for four days there had been cloud and drizzle.

At some point, however, Worley was back on course—only, it seems, to have another wanton and unnecessary change of plan. This time the testimony comes from messages sent ashore by a distinguished passenger on the *Cyclops*, the U.S. diplomat Alfred Gottschalk, and from accounts of the unscheduled stop made by Worley at Bridgetown, Barbados. On his way there, the mutinous atmosphere in the ship grew no better; nor did Worley's mental health, for in addition to his violent switches of mood, he was now drinking to excess. "Always a heavy drinker, by now he'd gone over the top," according to one report.

What made him call at Barbados has never been discovered. His ship was fully provisioned, and laden with enough coal to see him direct to Baltimore. Yet something—his disturbed mind?—persuaded him to break the journey. Contact was made with the United States consul, Brokholst Livingston. Although Worley seems to have had a brief respite from the worst of his manic moods during the visit, Livingston took an instant, suspicious dislike to the Commander.

Much against his will, Livingston personally paid out $775 on Worley's behalf for a ton of fresh meat, a ton of flour, and 1,000 pounds of vegetables. Worley himself, having requested 600 tons of coal, eventually took on 1,500 tons. Livingston was well aware of the irrationality. Why was Worley apparently short of money? Why the needless extra coal? If extra provisions were needed, why —relatively speaking—did he take so little (for what he took on would not go far among the 309 crew and passengers on board)?

Worley departed after 48 hours, and as he did so, he laid a further trail of confusion. It was noted that the ship did not fly the traditional homeward-bound pennant, and in fact steamed *south*. Worley had told Livingston that he was headed for Bermuda, in the opposite direction. Even so, why Bermuda? A safer course would have taken him much closer to the Straits of Florida, where he would have had the benefit of the northward-running Gulf Stream. The next day, March 5, he radioed the British liner *Vestris* to say that he was on course and in good weather. But on course to where?

Nobody knows. That is the last that was heard from Worley or his ship. By March 13 the *Cyclops* was noted as being overdue, and a massive, totally fruitless search took place. To this day there is no satisfactory explanation of what happened, and although this is not yet the place to speculate on what *may* have happened to her, it is perhaps worth noting that the one common element in all the reconstructions that have been written about this last voyage is the strange behavior of Worley and the related, doom-laden atmosphere aboard the ship.

At this distance in time, it is not possible to make an exact correlation between the changing climatic conditions and Worley's worsening mental health —and in fact, even if it were possible to do so, the current state of knowledge about the effect of small magnetic changes on human behavior is so incomplete that it might not get us very far. However, broadly speaking, we can say that a connection seems to have existed in Worley's case. If this is so, what other clues can we uncover from contemporary research that may have a bearing on the disappearances that continue to take place within the Triangle today?

So far as the khamsin-type winds are concerned, great advances have been made since the discovery that they are, to use the right technical phrase, positively ionized. Air ionization is a term applied to molecules of air which carry a tiny amount of positive or negative electricity. Most air molecules are not electrically charged; in fact, only 4,000 in every two million million million are found to be charged in clean mountain air, and very much fewer in city air. Air ions are a natural phenomenon, but although atmospheric electricity has been known to science for at least 200 years, it is only during the last 20 years that its important influence on all forms of organic life has been recognized.

The normal ratio of negative to positive ions is 1.2:1. What happens in the khamsin and similar winds is that the ratio becomes reversed; just how this happens is not altogether known, for the positive ionization happens two days *before* the wind arrives, remains high for the first day of the wind, and then drops away as the temperature goes up and the dry heat of the wind begins to reduce the humidity.

Apparently what occurs during this time in the human body is that the sharp rise in the amount of positive ions in the air causes a hormone called serotonin to be produced, and this in turn is associated with the nervous system and with tension.

Some additional symptoms of hyper-production of serotonin include sleeplessness, irritability, tension, migraine, nausea and vomiting, impairment of vision, and swelling of tissue.

For most people—not all—these symptoms can quickly be reversed by charging the air artificially with negative ions, a treatment pioneered by Professor Felix Gad Sulman at the Hebrew University in Jerusalem. In the USSR and in Germany, ionization therapy is widely used in hospital practice, since research has shown that an enormous number of other benefits are produced—faster healing, reduction of the bacterial content of the air, analgesic effects. In the United States, clinical practice has tended to lag behind experimental results; it is certainly an area of applied science in which, for once, America does not lead the world.

The relevance of this work to the Triangle is evident, and perhaps dramatically important, if only because of the observed positive ionization in those sea areas known as the doldrums. *Doldrums,* after all, has the two dictionary meanings of (a) a dull, listless state of boredom, and (b) the becalmed area of any near-tropical sea where the trade winds negate each other—the latter a perfect description of those deceptively calm days, "weather fair," in the Triangle when vessels and planes have inexplicably disappeared. In such conditions positive ions predominate, as opposed to the health-giving negative ion areas that also occur naturally, such as the Yosemite Valley in the United States where, the Stanford Research Institute has found, the famous waterfalls generate a large negative charge.

Dr. E. Stanton Maxey, a scientist, surgeon, and

flight instructor, feels strongly that not enough attention is being paid to the problem. In a letter to the Editor of *Aviation Week and Space Technology* in May 1972, he says that doldrum conditions are enough to put some people into a trance-like state, causing accidents which are otherwise unexplained, and that cockpit devices should be installed to rectify the situation.

All the above is consistent with what we know of the weather which the *Cyclops* steamed into—variously described as "balmy," "still," "humid," "fair." There is a further clue in the sleepless habits of Commander Worley; abnormal quantities of serotonin are known to affect the sleep-wake cycle.

While this does not yet provide an answer for the disappearance of the *Cyclops* itself, it throws new light on the background before the disappearance; and as the investigation found later, the mysterious process by which serotonin is produced within the body has a fascinating and perhaps crucial link with the way that some people seem to be able to move themselves—and sometimes physical objects, too—into another dimension, thus providing a link with another aspect of the Triangle mystery. At this stage, however, it is only necessary to consider it as one of the strange and little-understood effects of electromagnetism on human behavior, and one which has a potential application to several previously unsolved Triangle mysteries.

There is, for example, the ten-day period in 1969, from June 30 to July 10, which even skeptics find mystifying. During this time no fewer than five boats were found to be abandoned or wrecked: the celebrated yachtsman Donald Crowhurst's *Teignmouth Electron* was found deserted, a rambling diary and intimations of suicide on board; the *Vagabond*, a 20-foot sloop found in perfect order by the Swedish ship *Golar Frost*; an unnamed 60-footer found floating bottom up by the British vessel *Maplebank*; a 35-foot yacht, set on automatic steering, with no crew on board, found by the British vessel *Cotopax*; and the 35-foot yacht found upturned by the British tanker *Helisoma* between Bermuda and the Azores. The best-investigated of these tragedies (that of Donald Crowhurst) shows unmistakable signs of the kind of lethargy and insanity induced by doldrum-type conditions. Crowhurst had almost certainly faked the entries in his log that would have showed him the leader in a round-the-world yacht race. His mind, according to two journalists who minutely researched the circumstances of his death, "gradually gave way." Did the same thing happen with the other victims during the same time period?

So far, we have established that these tiny ionization and hormonal changes—all of them a function of electromagnetism—have undisputed disorientation effects. At least temporarily, they can unhinge people's minds, even though scientists do not properly understand the mechanism that makes this happen. Accepting this does not make events in the Triangle any less mysterious, for the proposal that natural events can have seemingly supernatural consequences is itself unorthodox. What it does is to place the investigation on a footing which is based on facts, even if they are little-known facts.

So the next question is: What other discoveries are being made on the fringe of scientific knowledge that may help to provide a natural basis for explaining the Triangle mysteries? High among them must come two that again seem to have their basis in electromagnetism anomalies: ball lightning, and the macabre phenomenon known as spontaneous human combustion.

As with ionization effects, it has taken scientists a long time to agree that ball lightning even exists. The reason for denying it has again been that there is no scientific way of explaining its existence—and unless scientists can find a theoretical way of explaining something, they usually prefer to ignore it or deny it (as with the Triangle itself). Thus learned journals have printed academic explanations for the phenomenon that it is "spots before the eyes," or "after-images"—in other words, self-delusion by the witnesses.

Unfortunately, it is rather difficult to persuade the witness of this when he or she has been physically burned by a supposedly imaginary ball of fire. Take the case of a young housewife in the kitchen of her home in Smethwick, an industrial town in the center of Britain, in the summer of 1975. From nowhere, a sphere of light appeared over the stove. It was about four inches across, and surrounded by a flame-colored halo, colored bright blue to purple. The ball moved straight toward her, staying about three feet above the ground, too quickly for her to get out of the way. "The ball seemed to hit me below the belt, as it were, and I automatically brushed it from me and it just disappeared. Where I brushed it away there was a redness and swelling on my left hand. It seemed as if my gold wedding ring was burning into my fingers."

The ball went off with a bang and burned a hole in her skirt—evidence that was subsequently measured and discussed, so that calculations could be made about the quality of energy involved. In this case it was relatively small, but even so, enough to ignite an inflammable store such as a tanker of fuel. Typically, these spooky balls, usually spherical but sometimes pear-shaped, are one foot and upwards in diameter. They hover or bounce erratically, moving at a rate of around six feet per second, and their "life" has been observed as lasting from several seconds to several minutes. They often disappear with a loud bang and a smell of ozone, sulphur, or nitrogen.

So far as the Triangle is concerned, they are interesting because in appearance they are much like many of the UFO sightings that are frequently reported in the area—indeed, ball lightning is often called in as an explanation for UFOs generally (an example of a mystery being explained by something that is equally a mystery). At the same time, they are also linked—perhaps caused—by the kind of electromagnetic disturbance that seems to operate in the Triangle.

Exactly the nature of this disturbance is not yet known. Ball lightning most frequently occurs in the wake of cyclones and thunderstorms of the kind that plague the Triangle during the typhoon season; but equally, the fireballs can appear in broad daylight.

What makes them worrying to scientific theory, and unnerving to any normal observer, is the way that they can appear without warning *inside* cars, boats, ships, even sealed and pressurized planes. The effect is frighteningly ghost-like. Consider these two eyewitness accounts, both from respected journals.

About 50 years ago I was standing on the steps of a shop in Orford Place, Norwich, sheltering from a violent thunderstorm. In front of me stood a tram—empty. Suddenly a large fireball descended—I did not see from where—but it was the size of a large football. It passed through the rear apron of the tram, travelled the length of the tram inside and out through the front apron, and then exploded on the ground outside.

After the storm had subsided I got down from the steps and examined the tram. There was a large hole in the rear apron and also in the front apron.

This communication records the observation of ball lightning in unusual circumstances. I was seated near the front of the passenger cabin of an all-metal airliner (Eastern Airlines Flight EA 539) on a late night flight from New York to Washington. The aircraft encountered an electrical storm during which it was enveloped in a sudden bright and loud electrical discharge (0005 h EST, March 10, 1963). Some seconds after this a glowing sphere a little more than 20 cm in diameter emerged from the pilot's cabin and passed down the aisle of the aircraft approximately 50 cm from me, maintaining the same height and course for the whole distance over which it could be observed.

My account tallied precisely with that of the only other occupant of the passenger cabin, a terrified air hostess who was strapped in her seat on the opposite side and farther to the rear of the aircraft. She saw the ball continue to travel down the aisle and finally disappear towards the lavatory at the end. I had no alcohol on this flight.

Just how often these weird events take place is another cause of scientific wrangling. A survey of NASA personnel suggested it might be fairly frequent—"nearly as frequent as ordinary cloud-to-ground strokes." But it is rarely photographed. Only six out of 100,000 photographs examined by scientists at Wyoming University in 1975 had ball-like qualities. Even so, one can extrapolate from this an annual total the world over of perhaps 300,000, of which a significant number must surely occur in the Triangle.

Various estimates have been made of their energy content, none of them especially high. There are 17th-century accounts of men and women being killed by ball lightning, but it is not clear whether associated lightning strokes may not themselves have caused the death. However, even these relatively low estimates, such as that causing the burning of the Smethwick housewife's skirt, can be catastrophic in the wrong circumstances. Two scientists from the Amoco Oil Research Department have listed some of the occasions in the last ten years in which otherwise safe transporters were turned into infernos.

1. Distillate was being loaded into the open top of an 8,000-gallon transport truck when "a ball of light travelled along the fill pipe and down the droptube. It entered the truck compartment and the truck blew up."

2. Solvent was being loaded through closed piping into the bottom of a 7,600-gallon transport truck when "a ball of light followed along the fill

toward the truck and disappeared. Then the truck blew up."

3. Jet fuel was being loaded into the open top of a transport truck. "A ball of light entered the truck compartment and it blew up."

4. A retired New York City fireboat captain, Charles Wilson of Codan Marine Inc., New York, told of three cases where "a ball of light was reported to have moved across the deck of a barge just before the barge blew up."

5. A tanker captain with the same corporation, Captain Wykoff, reportedly "saw a ball of light move across the deck toward a compartment before it blew up."

6. An observer on a ship several miles from a VLCC (very large crude carrier) tanker reported that "a ball of light travelled along the deck of the ship and disappeared. Then the ship blew up."

The authors of this report say that "taken individually, these instances are each incredible and are usually ignored by safety experts." But collectively, they are powerful evidence, and once again it is easy to see how a little-known, sometimes derided scientific occurrence might well be the initial cause of a number of Triangle disappearances.

In April 1974 the 54-foot trawler yacht *Saba Bank* disappeared during its shakedown cruise in the Caribbean. The yacht was seaworthy and almost unbelievably well equipped. It vanished without trace between Nassau and Miami, Florida, and there is still a reward for its discovery. Although hijacking has been put forward as a possible reason for its loss, the passage of time without its distinctive design having been recognized anywhere in the world makes this solution increasingly unlikely. Its specially enlarged fuel tanks, however, would have been particularly vulnerable to any fire source able to penetrate the vessel.

Then there are the mysterious cases of the three sulphur-carrying ships: the *Hewitt*, which disappeared after sailing from Sabine, Texas, in January 1921 after being sighted about 250 miles north of Jupiter Inlet, Florida; the 3,337-ton bulk carrier *Southern District* that vanished in December 1954 somewhere in the Gulf of Mexico with a crew of 23 on board; and the classic case of the *Marine Sulphur Queen*, a 425-foot freighter last seen 270 miles off Florida Keys. In the last, investigated at length but inconclusively by the U.S. Coast Guard Marine Board of Investigation, a fire and explosion on board has been one of the preferred explanations. But with the safeguards built into the ship's operational procedure and design, the cause of such a fire has been difficult to imagine. With ball lightning, one is readily to hand.

In another of those sets of coincidences that plague an investigation of the Bermuda Triangle, it was nine years to the day that another ship of the same sort carrying exactly the same number of passengers (39) sank in 150 feet of water in the Gulf of Mexico. The tanker—the *V. A. Fogg*—was on a short journey to flush out her tanks and return. As this routine operation was carried out, something caused the volatile benzene to explode, quickly sinking the vessel and creating a 10,000-foot-high column of black smoke that eventually brought rescuers to the site, although too late to save any lives. Was the spark that ignited the blaze a fireball? In the context of what we now know about them, the possibility can certainly not be discounted.

As we have seen, science has not been able to come up with an agreed explanation for these mysterious balls of fire. Specifically, the mystery of how they hold themselves together for a visible period of time is for the moment inexplicable. However, the phenomenon is undoubtedly linked with the kind of magnetic changes that exist during thunderstorms, and may itself be electromagnetic. The scientist who saw the remarkable example of ball lightning inside the New York–Washington airplane thinks it is dependent on "the phase-locked loop of electromagnetic radiation in the intense field associated with lightning activity . . . There is, in these circumstances, a particular wavelength of electromagnetic radiation which can form a stable standing wave which externally exhibits a spherical configuration and which excites the ambient gas to produce the glow by which it is seen."

In other words, this part of the investigation again moved toward the rarer properties of electromagnetism as an indication of how to explain Triangle mysteries. This led to an even stranger phenomenon: spontaneous human combustion. With it came the first clue that electromagnetism, on top of causing mental derangement, might be responsible for actual disappearances (the second aspect of the triple Triangle mystery).

As a phenomenon, spontaneous human combustion is even less well regarded in the scientific community than ball lightning—and certainly, the two have not so far been brought together in respectable scientific journals in the same way as, for instance, the ball lightning interpretation of UFOs formed so large a part of the U.S. Government's Condon Report. It is gruesome, which may account for some people's distaste for investigating it. But another reason, once again, is the scientist's reluctance even to consider an event whose cause is outside the general body of scientific theory.

The visible effects of spontaneous human combustion are easy enough to describe. The "corpse" consists of a small pile of greasy ash, almost always with an extremity—a hand, a foot—left untouched by whatever caused the body to disintegrate. Around the remains there is usually (but not always) localized charring. It is not known how often the event occurs. It was widely noted in Victorian times, and was mentioned in books by Zola, Marryat, Melville, de Quincey, and Dickens. In this century, there have been some two dozen unquestionable cases, but these are almost certainly just the tip of the iceberg, for coroners and fire officers are likely to attribute many of the deaths to normal fires.

"Normal" fire is the one thing that spontaneous human combustion certainly isn't. Here are just two of the "impossibilities":

No cremation consumes the human body so completely. Dr. Wilton M. Krogman, Professor of Physical Anthropology at the University of Pennsylvania's School of Medicine, and an internationally reputed forensic scientist, has observed that the normal cremation procedure involves a temperature of 3,000° Fahrenheit over a period of some 12 hours. Even so, there are always calcined fragments of bone. In the fierce heat that follows, say, the burning of an automobile wreck, the skeletal structure of the occupants is readily recognizable. Yet in spontaneous human combustion often all that remains is the small heap of blue-gray ash.

Fire damage is inexplicably confined to the immediate area. In most cases, no damage is found more than a yard or so from what is left of the body. The *British Medical Journal* of 21 April 1888 gives an account of a pensioner in Aberdeen, Scotland, who was last seen on an evening in February climbing into a hayloft above a stable. He fell asleep, somewhat drunk, and the next morning his body was discovered "almost a cinder. Both hands and the right foot had been burnt off and had fallen through the floor among the ashes into the stables below . . . There had been no death struggle. The man had expired without suffering, the body burning away quietly all the time. . . .

"The strange fact remains that while round about in close proximity were dry woodwork and hay, loose and in bundles, these had escaped, and the body of the man was thoroughly incinerated."

The same writer, Dr. J. Mackenzie Booth, remarks that many other cases were known where, remarkably, "the bodies were burnt and charred out of all proportion to the neighbouring objects, and to an extent which seems incapable of being accounted for by the heat of the burning clothes and objects in the vicinity." In this century, there have been rare cases where even the clothing has not been damaged; it is as if a fire has been started from inside the body, worked its way outwards, and then stopped on coming into contact with normal combustible material. At the inquest on Mrs. Stanley Lake at Kingston, New York, reported in the *New York Sun* of January 24, 1930, the coroner concluded: "Although her body was severely burned, her clothing was not even scorched."

How many Triangle disappearances may have been triggered off by this phenomenon cannot be known; but there is no reason why it should not have been a factor in some of the mysterious cases reported as much as a century ago, where ships such as the *Rosalie* were found deserted apart from a few starving cats and canaries (animals and birds have never been witnessed as victims of spontaneuos combustion), and even in airplane explosions that have been observed to occur without known cause.

However, rather than speculate on specific instances, it is more fruitful to consider the general implications as far as the Triangle is concerned. Firstly, spontaneous human combustion is a phenomenon that unquestionably has an electromagnetic basis, because of the heat involved. What part of the electromagnetic spectrum this comes from is unlikely to be those radiations that we see as flames, for otherwise the surroundings would burn up as completely as the bodies. The most likely place is a little lower in the spectrum, among the microwaves. In just the same way as a microwave oven cooks internally—from the inside outward, without immediate harm to the protective skin—what starts off human combustion must work in a somewhat similar way.

Secondly, it is possible that balls of lightning, in themselves not very powerful sources of exterior burning, might work in this way. If the "phase-locked loop of electromagnetic radiation" invoked by some scientists as an explanation for ball lightning happens to lie in the microwave region, this effect would be theoretically possible. In much the same way as a fireball is capable of igniting tankers of petroleum gas, it might equally be able to trigger off irreversible electromagnetic combustion in the body.

Thirdly, a deeply fascinating connection has been made between the occurrence of spontaneous human combustion and the kind of magnetic changes that seem to accompany both ball lightning and the ionization effects that cause disorientation and mental instability. The U.S. writer and scientific investigator Livingston Gearhart decided to check up what the worldwide state of magnetic activity was at the time when these strange combustions took place. His basic data were compiled from the readings taken each day by the U.S. National Oceanic and Atmospheric Administration in Boulder, Colorado; observatories all over the world send in readings of the earth's magnetic field strength in their area, and these are then combined to provide a global average for that particular day. The scale goes in decimal points from 0 (quiet) to 2 (magnetic storm). The six cases which he chose as a sample, in each of which he was able to establish accurately the time of death, coincided with a sharp increase in global magnetic activity.

Fourthly, spontaneous human combustion joins the growing list of electromagnetic phenomena which science is at a loss to explain. From now on, the investigation into what may be going on in the Bermuda Triangle moves into increasingly mysterious, though connected, areas. Just how is it that the human body can sense these tiny changes? Is there a link between electromagnetism and other levels of consciousness, other dimensions, even?

It is well to remember that if scientists cannot understand these relatively well-observed phenomena, we should not be too worried if they are even more reluctant to accept some of the so-called psychic occurrences that must also be examined before any solution to the Triangle mystery emerges. Strange events may require strange explanations.

CHAPTER THREE

Human Radio

Guests at the Ambergris Cay Hotel on Grand Turk island were enjoying their pre-dinner cocktails on a hot June evening in 1969. It is a good hotel, the kind the British call "smooth," and as they gossiped, they were mildly irritated for a full half-hour by the drilling buzz of a little Cessna 172 flying back and forth, apparently aimlessly, 600 feet overhead.

There were, the investigation subsequently found, 42 hotel guests in the bar and on the terrace that night. Not one knew there was a strange, disordered drama going on above.

The pilot of the small plane was Caroline Coscio, a Miami Beach nurse, on her way with her boyfriend from Pompano Beach, Florida, to the Bahamas. She had refueled at Georgetown, and was due to do the same on Grand Turk when the airstrip control tower operator there heard a disturbing report from her: "I'm lost. My direction equipment isn't functioning. Can anyone down there help me?"

The operator assumed the airplane above was hers, and offered assistance. Apparently she could not hear him. Her voice could be heard talking to her boyfriend. He, too, was confused. "Where are we?" "How should I know? You're the pilot."

The snatches of conversation that came over the radio grew increasingly deranged. "We must have taken a wrong turn. That can't be Turk—there's nothing there."

This in spite of the evident activity on the island that could surely be seen from a height of only 600 feet, with the evening lights from the many hotels, houses, and highways beginning to be switched on and sparkle through the dusk.

And then another evident contradiction: "I'm circling two islands—there's nothing down there."

A few minutes later, by now away from the coastline and out to sea, she called, "I'm out of fuel and I'm sinking. . . . Is there no way out of this?"

Nothing more was heard after her final message at 8:22 p.m., and the Coast Guard station at Miami Beach was alerted immediately. It is the busiest and most successful in the world, handling 12,000 distress calls a year. Within half an hour there was an unidentified report that a Cessna, presumably hers, had been spotted in the water 60 miles north of Monte Cristo, twelve miles northwest of Grand Turk. Two Coast Guard cutters and a helicopter sped to the site. Seven H-16 seaplanes were on standby, with a further cutter available if needed. The helicopter first at the site reported that there was now nothing to be seen.

By dawn next day the full search operation was put into effect. Besides the craft above, there were three huge C-131 cargo planes, capable of many hours in the air, and two more long-range helicopters. All were used, to no avail. Once again, there was a disappearance that left no wreckage, and no clues apart from the ambiguous and disturbed radio interceptions.

Reviewing the Caroline Coscio case during our investigation, it was plain that it showed two of the classic elements of the Triangle mystery in general—disorientation, and apparent disappearance of solid objects. We decided to pursue the line that somehow an explanation for these two "impossible" events must lie in the many little-known effects of electromagnetism and decided to see if any of the naturally occurring magnetic anomalies that have been recorded within the Triangle might in some way be relevant.

Nobody denies that both magnetic and climatic anomalies exist there, and in the surrounding area. The *Admiralty Pilot,* the "bible" of international navigation, records a number of persistent ones:

CHART 360: Local magnetic anomaly, causing abnormal variation that varies from an increase of 2° to a decrease of 5° from the normal, has been observed over and in the vicinity of Plantagenet Bank.

CHARTS 332, 334, 868: From time to time observations on the Bermuda Islands for variation, dip and horizontal force have given values differing considerably from those which might be expected from the position of the group in the earth's magnetic field.

The irregularities reported by HMS *Challenger* in 1873 have been fully confirmed by a considerable number of observations subsequently obtained.

Some idea of the scale of anomaly sometimes occurring at sea can be gathered from occasional reports in the *Marine Observer:*

3:55 p.m. December 23rd, 1928 . . . both compasses were suddenly deflected 90°, North Point switching to East, and then swung freely back to normal. Period of disturbance about three minutes.

From the Meteorological Log of SS *Elpenor*, Captain A.L. Gordon:

30th March, 1937, 0217 GMT . . . a magnetic disturbance was experienced. The compass suddenly became very erratic, at one time pointing as much as 20° to the east of magnetic north. Within two minutes the compass-card settled down, and an azimuth showed the error to be normal again.

It is, of course, possible to argue that the calmly noted aberrations appearing in the various logs prove that experienced sailors, in a rational frame of mind, are able to overcome the temporary effects of magnetic changes and indeed to record and report them subsequently. This is self-evident. But as we have seen earlier, magnetic changes do *not* always allow a rational state of mind to continue; the cases of mental instability linked with the approach of certain storms show that some people find magnetic effects irresistible.

Moreover, it is now certain that a sense of magnetism is built into us all. The Earth itself, for reasons that scientists do not pretend to understand, is a giant but weak magnet, and NASA space probes have collated the subtle shifts and changes that occur over its surface. The magnetic field strength is strongest at the poles and weakest near Rio de Janeiro. The gradation is not consistent over the whole of the Earth's surface, and it fluctuates a little day by day. The area covered by the Bermuda Triangle is usually about midway in strength.

Of course we do not consciously sense this magnetic field, any more than we feel anything if we put a finger inside a child's horseshoe magnet (which is, incidentally, at least one thousand times more powerful than the field created by the Earth). But this weak field is intricately linked with the ionization effects mentioned at the beginning of this book, and it is becoming steadily clearer that it is not the actual strength of the field, but the *changing* strength, which is important to human life.

If this is so—and as we found out, many good physicists believe it to be the case—then the magnetic anomalies in the Triangle, the small variations derided by many orthodox scientists as an insignificant factor in the many disappearances, suddenly take on a new importance.

So just what is the evidence? Much of the research in this area has come from a handful of physicists who have taken it upon themselves to find out how the art of dowsing, or water-witching, can be explained. What these physicists were interested in finding out was whether there could be an anatomical explanation for the way the dowser's rod twitched or moved, also what caused the movement.

The first question proved the simplest to work out. It seems that unconscious neuromuscular reactions can provide the momentum for the bending of a hazel twig or the galloping rotation of a pendulum. Although some people have suggested a psychokinetic, or other-dimensional, force that involuntarily moves the rod, they are in a minority. Apparently most people can experience what happens, if they are taught to hold the rod the right way.

What causes the unconscious muscular movement in the first place is a more difficult question to answer. However, it is more than a coincidence that the two most likely causes are precisely those that offer themselves as a solution in the case of the Triangle itself: (a) magnetic field changes and (b) contact with another dimension of knowledge.

In other words, what the scientists (much to their surprise) are uncovering in their research into dowsing can apply equally to the unseen forces that must lie at the heart of the Triangle disappearances.

Taking the work on magnetism first, the basic research on this was done in the 1940s and 1950s by Professor Solco W. Tromp, the Dutch geologist, who showed in a massive series of experiments—his book, *Psychical Physics*, is 534 pages in length—that when dowsers walked over an artificially created magnetic field, their rods moved abruptly.

This pioneering finding was refined and improved by Yves Rocard in 1963. Professor of Physics at the Ecole Normale in Paris (the leading

French college of teachers) and a member of the French Atomic Energy Commission, he showed that while Tromp was right, both dowsers and amateur "witchers" could detect magnetic field changes much smaller than Tromp had suggested.

Finally there has been the work of Dr. Zaboj Harvalik on behalf of the American Society of Dowsers. Also a physicist with an eminent academic background, having been Professor of Physics at the University of Arkansas, his experiments have a sophisticated simplicity to them, for all he asked people to do was to walk over a patch of ground, dowsing rod in hand, while he noted whether the rods moved or not.

What his subjects did not know was that beneath the ground was a minute amount of electric current, which a random number generator switched on and off. On the surface of the ground, this current showed itself as a tiny magnetic anomaly (about the same amount as would be produced by an underground stream running through rock).

Dr. Zaboj Harvalik's results have been stunning. He has shown that 90 percent of us can detect a magnetic variation *ten thousand times* weaker than the Earth's own magnetic field. In the case of his best subject, the German master dowser Wilhelm de Boer, this figure increased in sensitivity to an incredible *one billion times*.

It means, according to one authority interpreting his results, that "we are all living, breathing, sensors of magnetic change—human magnetometers probably even more sensitive than the best that the most advanced electronics manufacturers can produce."

If Zaboj Harvalik's results are correct (and they

have been extracted from nearly ten years' research including subjects from the U.S. Defense Department), it means that the kind of magnetic anomaly existing in the Triangle and elsewhere may well be responsible for some of the strange decisions made by people flying and sailing in the area.

For instance, it has long been noted that the Bermuda Triangle is one of the few places on Earth where compass north and true north are identical. Now, under "normal"—that is to say, artificial—navigational conditions, this would supposedly make navigation easier: instead of having to allow a compass variation in plotting position and direction, what the compass reads is in fact accurate.

But suppose that at the moment of cross-over, the moment when true and magnetic north coincide, something within the pilot's body unconsciously recognizes this? What disorienting effects —again, unconscious—might this have? For it is absolutely certain that if, as Dr. Harvalik has shown, we can recognize these tiny magnetic field changes, we can also unconsciously recognize where the direction of the poles lies; and indeed, in his own experiments, and in experiments with animals and other forms of life that we shall come to in a moment, it has been shown time and again that this sense of direction is innate, and that only the complications of modern society and machinery have prevented our realizing this.

There is, for example, the classic mystery of the after-Christmas DC-3 flight in 1948 from San Juan, Puerto Rico, that should have ended up safely in Miami—a flight precisely along one of the three sides of the Bermuda Triangle—but in fact never arrived, vanishing, it seems, only 50 miles from its destination at precisely one of these magnetic "cross-over" points.

Of all the aircraft of any type ever built, the DC-3 is conceded to be the most durable and reliable. Of 10,000 DC-3s built between 1935 and 1947, some 2,000 were still flying in 1977. On this occasion, the DC-3 concerned had flown for twelve years without incident, and was in the hands of a pilot with an equally good record for reliability—the eminently sane Captain Robert Linquist, with 3,265 hours' flying time. His co-pilot, Ernest Hill, had logged 197 hours; the stewardess, Mary Burke, was highly experienced and later described as having "indestructible cheerfulness." So there was nothing in either the airplane or the crew to presage disaster.

However, a fresh look at the Civil Aviation Board's Accident Investigation Report reveals that there were a few hints of omens, of possible electromagnetic malfunctioning. As the 27 passengers, two of them babies, waited in the small airport lounge for Linquist to take on fuel (he had already flown the outward leg earlier in the day), they were delayed while the landing gear locking device was inspected. As Linquist suspected, his batteries were a little low, causing the warning locklight not to come on. He ordered the batteries to be topped up and then taxied the empty airplane to test its radio capability.

The local Chief of Aviation was called to the scene to confirm the DC-3's reliability. Linquist told him, "My receiver is functioning, but the transmitter seems out. Everything else checks okay."

Without two-way radio communication, Linquist could not fly on an instrument flight plan. The

Chief of Aviation granted his request to file a visual flight plan instead, on the condition that he fly a few circuits of San Juan to top up the battery power.

This was agreed. It meant delaying the flight by two hours, but at the end of this time the pilot and the authorities had satisfied themselves that the DC-3 met all reasonable safety standards.

Ten minutes after takeoff, Linquist was flying his holding pattern as ordered by the Aviation Chief. Radio communication was established satisfactorily, and Linquist was on his way. The flight was scheduled to take six and three-quarter hours. There was enough fuel for a further three quarters of an hour. The weather was fine, with unlimited visibility. En route, Linquist and the DC-3 were picked up, correctly scheduled, by the Royal Air Force base at Kingston in the British West Indies and by other air bases.

Then at 04:13 came the last message—a mysterious one for a number of reasons. Firstly, it was picked up not by Miami, but by airport control center in New Orleans, 850 miles *farther on*. Yet Linquist himself was in no doubt that he was nearing Miami: "We are approaching the field fifty miles south."

So he was virtually on his final approach when he disappeared—certainly well within his scheduled landing time half an hour later, having caught up some time with a following wind for part of the trip. What then happened to him, his crew, his DC-3, and the passengers, has never been established. A massive hunt that started at first light found nothing, in spite of the fact that the water in the area indicated by Linquist is clear and shallow.

Only two things can conceivably have occurred.

Either Linquist, for all his experience, was nowhere near where he thought and said he was—in which case some unseen magnetic or electromagnetic influence must have brought about a massive navigational failure in himself or in the aircraft's instruments.

Or somehow the DC-3 and its occupants slipped literally into another dimension.

Once again, science shows us that the two things—even a combination of both—are not impossible. The best way to look at this is to examine the enigma of animal and bird migration, and in particular the curious aspect of migration that is known as homing. In their study of this phenomenon, scientists have come to realize that, just as Zaboj Harvalik has found with his dowsers, many creatures have senses (super-senses, you might call them) that are unimaginable by the conscious human mind. Some fish can detect temperature differences of as little as 0.03°C, and it has been speculated that this is how eels from Europe and America keep on course to the Sargasso Sea in the heart of the Bermuda Triangle; the Europe/Sargasso temperature gradient rises from 10°C to 40°C. Several fish found in West African rivers, for instance *gymnarchus niloticus*, generate their own electric field, and are highly sensitive to minute electromagnetic signals—the equivalent, say, of being able to spot a fading flashlight bulb a mile away. Many fish have an extraordinarily acute sense of smell, which is supposed to account for how salmon can identify the mouth of the river from which they migrated shortly after being born, and return to it for breeding. Another ability shared by many insects and birds, but not man or mammals, is to see the sky as if through a polarized lens. To a bee, a patch of cloudless sky does not look uniformly blue, but like a pattern of alternating light and dark stripes, as if you were looking through polarized sunglasses at an automobile windshield. Birds are known to use the sun as if it were a compass, and the stars at night as a map with which to guide their way.

All this is a deeply fascinating demonstration of just how sensitive and finely attuned all living things are to the world we live in. But for investigators of the Triangle mystery, and the problem of why such experienced people as Robert Linquist should apparently become completely disoriented, the truly significant finding by scientists is that migratory route-finding is only *partly* dependent on measurable sensory cues such as these.

Other factors are operating as well—and it is more than a coincidence that the most important of them are magnetism, and the idea of another dimension.

Take magnetism first, since it is at least partly understood in theory. It has now been proved that in heavily overcast conditions, when pigeons are unable to use any direct sighting cues and even their ability to make use of polarized light is negated, they switch over to route-finding by an inner magnetic compass. Carefully controlled experiments have shown that if small magnets are attached to the pigeons the wrong way round, so that north is south and vice versa, the pigeons become hopelessly confused. Another proven example of magnetic sensitivity is the miraculous bee-dance, in which worker bees returning from a source of nectar are able to communicate its location to other bees by performing a complicated series of maneuvers on the honeycomb. If the magnetic field around the honeycomb is artificially altered, the dance becomes a meaningless series of patterns. As with pigeons, robins, and gulls, an unknown sensory organ within the bee is directly responsive to the Earth's magnetism, and when this is interfered with the result is mental confusion.

Of course it is a large step to move from this to the confused behavior of pilots in the Bermuda Triangle, but the significant thing is that all this is a very recent research development; what can already be said is that the effect of magnetism, and magnetic changes, is incalculable, and should therefore certainly not be dismissed as a partial cause of strange human behavior.

The thoughts of scientists concerning the "other-dimensional" aspect of migration are even more directly compelling. Current opinion is that after making every allowance for physical aspects of route-finding—sun, stars, temperature, magnetism and so on—there must still be something else operating. The salmon's sense of smell may be satisfactory as a way of finding a river-mouth in Britain when it approaches within a few miles, but how does it know which direction to take for the two thousand miles and more from its natural habitat in the open sea? Distances covered can be vast—from Alaska to Korea in one example—but the direction-finding is infallible. The green turtles of Brazil are perhaps even more remarkable. Every two or three years they set off from the coast of southern America and find their way some 1,400 miles to the tiny target of Ascension Island, just five miles across; they never miss. And how did a lone Manx Shearwater, taken in a darkened container by airplane across the Atlantic to Boston,

Massachusetts, find its way back 3,000 miles to its nesting place on the island of Skokholm off the coast of Wales in just twelve and a half days?

The big question is not just how they do this, but why, and scientists have been forced to the conclusion that what happens is irresistible. The creatures are caught in an overwhelming tidal urge that drives them unavoidably to their destination. They "know" where to go partly because they have a shared inherited memory, but also partly because they are drawing on a pool of "cosmic information." One scientist explained it as if "birds, animals and insects are in the grip of an inexplicable cosmic current that is built into them through heredity and which most are unable to resist. That is why some creatures such as lemmings occasionally embark on a suicidal migration and decimate their numbers. It must also be why some birds will perish when the cold weather comes early rather than fly south, because the annual appointed day for their migration has not yet arrived."

So far as the Bermuda Triangle is concerned, this is a highly significant point of view. Serious scientists are now saying what they have always been reluctant to admit—that creatures can get caught up in a cosmic force beyond our understanding. The word "cosmic," used in this sense, could just as easily be replaced by "psychic," or "other-dimensional." The point is that something outside science is operating, *and it cannot be resisted.* Evidence is steadily mounting that the homing factor in migration is spontaneous and involuntary; it does not require the imagination to be too far stretched to suppose that occasionally, and dangerously, the same kind of trance-like urge to travel in a preordained way may well up from the deep unconscious of a man's mind.

This is of course a troubling concept. But our investigation found the evidence mounting that it had to be considered as an explanation not just for Robert Linquist, but for many other strange areas of research where magnetism and electromagnetism were being seen as only a partial answer; in order to explain some of the events taking place under investigators' eyes at the outermost edges of scientific knowledge, the idea of a fifth dimension (or of many undiscovered dimensions) had to be postulated.

Take dowsing again.

In the most authoritative recent book on the subject, *Dowsing: The Psi Connection* (Anchor/Doubleday), the writer, Francis Hitching, concludes that while magnetic field changes can perhaps answer the previously unsolved mystery of how dowsers are able to detect underground water, it cannot answer some of the more extraordinary feats such as map-dowsing, in which the dowser, using nothing more than a map as a reference, is able to "divine" information.

He lists a large number of times when this has been successful, including a carefully controlled experiment where a dowser in the United Kingdom successfully pinpointed unknown archaeological sites in New England, and comments that this can only be explained by invoking some kind of "direct knowledge"—a way of extracting information from another dimension—since no known electromagnetic wave would be sufficiently powerful to carry a mental picture of the sites concerned. Other psychic phenomena such as clairvoyance, telepathy, and remote viewing may also use the same mechanism.

The relevance of this to the Triangle is that it is a field of serious research where the possibility of another dimension is actually admitted, unlike the restricting parameters of the physical sciences where everything is supposed to be explicable through the observed behavior of one of the four known forces—gravitational, electromagnetic, nuclear, and "weak." If there is indeed another level of consciousness, or another dimension, into which dowsers and others can switch themselves, then it is at least possible to argue that the same thing may be happening involuntarily to some victims of the Triangle.

But there is another way in which this idea of another dimension is relevant to the Triangle, which is the state of mind of the people concerned. Here again our investigation found that dowsing research, medical research, and the disoriented messages of Triangle victims all added up to form a scientific picture of small electromagnetic anomalies triggering off incomprehensible and perhaps uncontrollable effects.

Dowsers, it has been noted, need to go into a mild trance-like state when they are performing successfully over maps, a mental condition perhaps not dissimilar to the disorientation which has been suffered by some of the pilots who have lost their way in the Triangle. Dr. Zaboj Harvalik has also found that the most likely area in the brain which is activated during the dowsing process is the pineal gland.

The pineal gland, in turn, is (1) involved in the production of serotonin, the hormone noted in the previous chapter as being associated with the insanity brought on by khamsin-type winds, and the doldrum conditions in parts of the Triangle at certain times; (2) traditionally regarded, in Eastern religions, as the "third eye" or "ajna chakra" through which other states of consciousness (i.e., other dimensions) are reached.

So you can say that, conceivably, activation of the pineal gland through the kind of magnetic activity existing in the Triangle may be enough to allow people to burst through into another level of consciousness, or vice versa, allow another physical dimension to penetrate through to human activity. Modern chemistry provides some scientific backing for this.

The serotonin produced by the pineal gland is of the same chemical series of indole alkaloids that include such psychedelic drugs as LSD-25, psylocybin, DMT and bufotenine—the last being the active ingredient in toads that are proverbially used in witches' brews to produce the same disorienting, change-of-consciousness effect. The biologist John Bleibtrau has noted another attribute of serotonin that is significant: "Bananas and plums abound in serotonin; so do figs, and among species of figs none is richer than the *ficus religiosa,* under which the Buddha reportedly sat when he became enlightened."

Just how serotonin works within the body is not understood, for differing amounts of the hormone produce paradoxical effects. But it is entirely consistent with what is known to speculate that, as with dowsers and mystics going into some form of other-dimensional trance when the pineal gland is self-activated and excess serotonin is thereby produced, so those people unwittingly going through

79

the Triangle in anomalous electromagnetic or ionization conditions may similarly be affected.

In other words, the disorientation and derangement noted in such incidents as Flight 19 and the mental state of Commander Worley may be only the beginning of the story; the concept of another, serotonin-activated dimension must also be brought into the reckoning.

If this is the case, what categories of Triangle mysteries can tentatively be considered in this light? There are probably three:

1. All those mysteries where there is a clear sign of a muddled mental state by the people concerned immediately before the disaster.

2. All those mysteries where planes, ships, and people seem genuinely to have vanished without trace—the abrupt disappearances that leave no wreckage behind.

3. All those mysteries which might be called "ghostly"—the eerie appearances and disappearances that even to skeptical observers seem to conjure up the specter of another world.

Most of the cases considered so far in this book qualify for the first category, and it may be that mental disorientation *always* occurs before disappearance into another dimension; since the last hours or minutes of every vanishing ship and plane have not been recorded for posterity, nobody can be sure of this. However, it is worth noting that in more or less every case where an accurate log has been possible, this has been the case.

Bermuda Triangle mysteries in the second "vanish-without-trace" category are even more common. In October 1954 a U.S. Navy Constellation left Maryland for the Azores but never reached its destination, vanishing just north of the Triangle with 40 people on board. It carried two radio transmitters, but neither was used to send an SOS. A massive search by 200 planes failed to reveal any clues, and the later Board of Inquiry failed to agree on an official explanation for the loss. Bad weather hampered the later stages of the search, but unless the idea of another dimension is brought in, it remains mystifying how 40 trained personnel could totally disappear.

Another example might be the disappearance in January 1967 of a Beechcraft Bonanza. The pilot was Robert van Westenborg, a 35-year-old Miami business consultant, known locally both to friends and Federal Aviation Agency officials as being exceptionally cautious about flight safety. Something in his mental state that day prevented him, for the first time in his life, from filing a flight plan. His reported intention, during the flight, was to take photographs of the Southern Bell Telephone Company's new microwave relay station; one of the three passengers on board with him was in the public relations department of the company. Yet when he took off, he left his camera behind—another sign of mental disturbance?

The last that was seen of the blue-and-white plane was when it took off from Key Largo and headed out to sea. The search took on the pattern familiar to investigators of the Triangle disappearances, but none the less mystifying for being familiar. It lasted a full seven days, with the usual armada of ships and planes being called in to help, without the faintest clue, the least hint of wreckage ever being found.

Our investigation also re-examined two of the

classic Triangle tragedies, the disappearance of the two Tudor IV airliners almost exactly a year apart in 1948 and 1949; and here, too, the new scientific research linking electromagnetism and other dimensions was potentially illuminating.

On the first occasion, the airliner Star Tiger was flying in the early hours of January 30 on a flight from London to Kingston, Jamaica, due to land at Bermuda airport for refuelling. The plane was carrying 25 passengers and a crew of six, led by the redoubtable Captain Brian McMillan, a veteran of more than 3,000 hours of flying with the RAF during World War II. Anticipating headwinds, he had ordered the Star Tiger to be "filled to the gills" on the previous fuelling stop in the Azores. During the flight there was regular radio communication showing that everything was proceeding consistently and on schedule. Although the rising winds pushed the plane slightly off course, it was a routine job to correct this by taking an astral fix; at the inquiry afterwards it was said that an experienced navigator, taking a dead reckoning by the stars, "was unlikely to be in error by more than fifteen miles."

So there was no reason for the commission of inquiry to suppose that anything untoward was concealed in the last messages to be received from the Star Tiger between midnight and 3:15 a.m., when the operator requested a radio bearing from Bermuda and was given a 100 percent accurate one of 72°. The airplane's position was now known exactly, and because of the headwinds, the ETA (estimated time of arrival) had been changed from 3:56 a.m. to 5 a.m.

But no more was heard. The Star Tiger vanished from the sky—"truly a modern mystery of the air," as the researcher Lawrence Kusche has put it. In England later, the Court of Investigation set up by the British Ministry of Civil Aviation said that "no more baffling problem has ever been presented for investigation" and went on to comment that it could not do more than "suggest possibilities, none of which reaches the level even of probability . . . the fate of the Star Tiger must forever remain an unsolved mystery."

What puzzled the Court was not just the absence of wreckage, although the massive search that was undertaken would certainly have been expected to find something from such a well-equipped airliner, but that no explanation seemed in any way likely. The Court absolutely eliminated the following possible causes:

1. *Constructional defects.* The Tudor IVs were in many ways ahead of their time. Although withdrawn from passenger service the next year following the unnerving coincidence of a sister plane, the Star Ariel, also disappearing in the Triangle (see below), many others flew without incident on the far more technically risky Berlin Airlift.

2. *Meteorological hazards.* The increasing wind strengths had been allowed for by the crew.

3. *Errors of altimetry.* The equipment was sound.

4. *Mechanical failure of engines.* Tudor IVs had four engines, the 1,760 horsepower Rolls-Royce Merlin 632s. The airliner design was such that it could fly on any two of them. In any case, the sophisticated instrumentation would probably

have given advance warning of danger if one was faulty, and no hint of this came through the radio messages.

The Court also considered and rejected the following additional possibilities:

5. *Fire.* By 1948 a rare occurrence in airplanes, and this one was in any case equipped with fire extinguishers. And why no distress signal, for any fire takes some time to develop?

6. *Radio failure, followed by fire.* "Requires the coincidence of two improbabilities . . ." said the Court.

7. *Loss of control.* An *ad hoc* solution, as the pilot was experienced, and the incident would have been unique in the history of the aircraft.

8. *Fuel starvation.* Would have been noted and reported.

There remains the possibility of an explosion, perhaps caused by metal fatigue—but in this case floating debris would almost certainly have been found sooner or later, as happened in all cases where another type of British civil airplanes similarly in advance of their time, the jet-powered Comets, suffered a series of disasters some years later.

In other words, for there to be an "orthodox" explanation for this Triangle disappearance, it has to be supposed that the otherwise regular and normal flight of the Tudor IV suddenly dipped oceanwards and the airplane dived intact through the ocean surface and down to the bed without cracking up—a solution, you might think, at least as unlikely as those rejected out of hand by the inquiry.

However, what the Court was not able to consider, because the information and research were not available to them at the time, was the possibility of temporary instability to either crew or instrumentation, or both, brought on by the changing weather conditions. We have seen in the previous chapter how the gross effects of magnetic and ionization changes come *before* the onset of storms. In the case of the Star Tiger, the Court noted quite rightly that there were "no atmospheric disturbances of a serious kind which might cause structural danger to an aircraft, and there were no electrical storms." However, within 48 hours just these conditions were occurring with such severity that the air search had to be called off. We can therefore see with hindsight that the magnetic conditions at the time of the crash were highly volatile, and if the idea of another dimension is to be thought of in connection with this mystery, at least we know that the contemporary barometric conditions were conducive to what is known of such an event.

It is also interesting to note that, reading between the lines of the Court's conclusions, there are hints of the inexplicable man-machine interactions that our investigation had already touched on; they were to become steadily more important as more Triangle mysteries were re-examined. In confessing itself baffled as to the causes, the Court was in a sense prophetic about the nature of the many Triangle tragedies to come:

In all activities which involve the co-operation of man and machine two elements enter of very diverse character. There is the incalculable element of the human equation dependent upon imperfectly known factors; and there is the mechanical element subject to quite different laws. A breakdown may occur in either separately or in both in conjunction. Or some external cause may overwhelm man and machine.

Almost precisely a year later, on January 17, 1949, a sister plane to the victim of this mysterious tragedy met an uncannily similar fate. The Star Ariel took off from Kindley Field, Bermuda, at 8:41 a.m. in perfect weather, with a calm sea all the way to Kingston, Jamaica, where the flight was due to end some five and a half hours later. One hour after takeoff came the routine radio check from the pilot, Captain J. McPhee, reporting his height and position, in good visibility, dead on course.

After that, no more was heard. Captain McPhee should have reported back to ground control at least every hour and in fact had received permission to switch radio frequencies to that of Kingston. So it can be presumed that whatever happened to him, his crew, and the aircraft happened a few miles either side of a well-plotted straight route, the length of which was at the maximum one hour's flying time—about 180 miles in all. Yet in spite of this relatively narrow band of ocean being extensively searched for five days by an armada of ships and planes, no trace was found.

The subsequent inquiry was as unsatisfactory as it had been a year before, and simply concluded: "Through lack of evidence due to no wreckage having been found the cause of the accident to the Star Ariel is unknown." Re-examining the report, there is just one significant reference to electromagnetic difficulties that may have played a part, but which were not considered important at the time because the significance of such small changes was not then known: There were freak radio conditions, making it difficult to maintain constant contact with the aircraft. Could these have been the cause of a severe navigational/mental disorientation? Nowadays, an inquiry into a similar disaster would no doubt consider this explanation and call evidence about it. In the state of knowledge at the time when the Star Ariel vanished, it was not though relevant.

Our investigation uncovered one experienced and highly reliable witness who has no doubts on this score. Carlton W. Hamilton, Chief Airport Traffic Controller at Opalaka, Florida, has been involved in commercial aviation for some 35 years, including holding down such demanding jobs as Air Traffic Controller at Miami International Airport. There could, we felt, be no more trustworthy expert, and it is highly significant that he is personally convinced that radio communications and navigational equipment can be uniquely affected in certain Triangle conditions.

In support of this, he cites a previously unpublished disappearance that is particularly good evidence because of the clear-headed and professional way in which he was able to observe and report it.

"In the late 1940s I was working a mid-watch at Miami Tower with just one other person. The mid-watch is the midnight to eight a.m. watch, and around three a.m. I picked up the pilot of a C-46 light aircraft requesting permission to land. There were no other aircraft on my frequency except this one.

"He was en route from Bogota, Colombia, to Miami, and was handed to me by Miami Air Route Traffic Control Center descending from 8,000 to 6,000 feet.

"As it happened, I knew the particular pilot of this aircraft personally quite well. He was an experienced pilot who had flown that route many, many times. We chatted a bit, how the weather was, his altitude, just general conversation. He spoke about how he had spotted the coast of Florida, which would have made him no more than about forty miles out. There weren't so many lights in Miami then as now, but even so he was able to see them. There was unlimited visibility, with just a few scattered clouds and winds no more than ten knots.

"I should stress that this was a perfectly routine flight. After a bit we kind of ran out of things to say to each other, so I told him to call me again when he got down to 6,000 feet. That should have been a few minutes later, and when I didn't hear from him I tried to re-establish contact myself.

"There was no response. I called the aircraft several times; still no response. I had Miami Air Route Traffic Control center start calling the aircraft. No response there. We alerted Air Sea Rescue; we had several other military units call the aircraft. No further transmission was ever received.

"The only explanation I have is that the aircraft lost all its navigational equipment and in turn the pilot lost his visual reference to the shoreline and therefore flew the aircraft right on into the ocean. After many years of observation, I believe that there is some type of condition that exists from time to time in the so-called Devil's Triangle, whereby the navigational equipment of boats and aircraft is totally disrupted."

It took less than 15 minutes after the last conversation between Carlton Hamilton and the C-46 pilot for the various radio operators to realize that something was seriously wrong. Air Sea Rescue was in the area where the pilot was missing within half an hour. But nothing was found. As dawn came up, the clear, calm sea was found to be unruffled by the disappearance. Not even an oil slick was ever found.

Once again it was as if some electromagnetic malfunctioning had led to another dimension. Carlton Hamilton's own belief is that such events are triggered off from "mineral deposits under the water, along with the rotation of the Earth, the positions of the planets, and the atmospheric conditions at the time."

What our own investigation now discovered was perhaps even more intriguing—the possibility that it may be the action of the human mind that is the agency for these other-dimensional catastrophes. This next stage in the search led us away from the Triangle and into the laboratory to find out the answer to one question: Knowing as we do that magnetism can affect humans, can humans affect magnetism?

CHAPTER FOUR

The Psi Effect

Only the vivid blue eyes of Ingo Swann, fixing upon a new acquaintance with the directness of a sculptor sizing up his subject, give any idea that he has abilities beyond the reach of normal men and women. A prosperous, dapperly dressed New York artist who turns out haunting, psi-dominated pictures from his Bowery studio, his psychic talents are some of the most extraordinary in the world today.

But not just extraordinary—proved, as well. Together with the young British subject Matthew Manning, and (to perhaps a less well-observed extent) Uri Geller, he is one of the handful of people in the Western world whose ability to move solid objects without touching them has been demonstrated beyond the doubt of any reasonable person.

Until quite recently, this proof was not available, and it may be because of the historic association between paranormal events and fraud that they have not previously been much discussed in terms of the Triangle mystery. But once you accept the evidence of psychokinesis—that solid objects, electromagnetic equipment, and so on, can be demonstrably affected by the presence of certain human beings—then its link with some of the Triangle disappearances is a compelling one.

Our investigation decided to take a hard look at the evidence; we found a great deal of it totally convincing.

The day in June 1972 when Ingo Swann arrived at Stanford Research Institute in California furnished a good example. In New York, he had already demonstrated his ability to alter the temperature inside sealed and insulated thermos bottles as much as 25 feet away from his body. Now, he was going to make further exploration of his psychic potential under the keen scrutiny of the SRI, which had recently put the physicist Dr. Harold Puthoff in charge of the experimentation.

Ingo Swann startled Puthoff somewhat with the blunt way in which he announced his terms for being involved: "I don't intend to get mixed up in any experiment that has loopholes the critics can pick on—it would be a waste of my time." However, Dr. Puthoff was equal to the occasion. He had already sought and found a scientific measuring device that was in every way impervious to human interference, and he suggested to Swann that they move over to Stanford University, where it was kept under the surveillance of Dr. Arthur Hebard.

The piece of equipment concerned was what is known as a "squid"—a superconductive quantum interfero metric device. Its purpose was to detect quarks, the elusive tiny "building blocks" of nature, whose presence had not at that time been established. For the purposes of the Swann experiment, its usefulness was that it was highly sensitive, being able to detect changes of as little as one millionth of the Earth's magnetic field—"the electronic equivalent of a supersensitive magnetic compass needle" is how Dr. Puthoff describes it.

The equipment had been designed so that inside it there was a steadily decaying magnetic field, which showed up as a constant wiggly line—a sine wave—on a strip recorder. "If you can psychically poke around inside this instrument and change the magnetic field in some way, that would really be something," Dr. Puthoff told him.

Ingo Swann imagined that the device would be some sort of an instrument on a table, and when they went into the basement of the Varian Hall of Physics and saw a room full of pipes and equipment, he asked which bit of this confusing jumble he was supposed to concentrate on.

"I was totally stunned to be told that the quark detector could not be visually perceived since it was encased in an aluminium container and copper canister, as well as a superconducting shield, and in any case was buried some five feet beneath the floor in concrete. This information caused my own eyes to swirl a little. It was a breathless situation, and somehow I felt a little tricked.

"To sit in a laboratory and poke around at small thermistors sealed in thermos flasks was one thing; at least one could get a general idea of where the target was. But the small anger that had boiled up in me passed quickly; here indeed was an experiment almost as immaculate as any could be."

He said later that it was probably this brief state of shock that sufficiently altered his consciousness for the incredible results that were shortly to come. For what Ingo Swann then did was to concentrate on the inside of the squid, trying to perceive through the darkness what its structural elements were.

As he did so, the sine wave doubled in frequency for about 30 seconds—an extraordinary thing to happen, and extremely dismaying to the inventor of the equipment, Dr. Arthur Hebard, who was watching, for the whole purpose of the squid was that it should be impenetrable to outside influences. Although the strip recorder had been running continuously for two hours previously without a tremor, the only scientific explanation Hebard could put forward for this sine wave aberration, almost jokingly, was some kind of unidentified "noise." So he decided to put Ingo Swann to an even more severe test. He asked him if it was possible to stop the sine wave for, say, ten seconds.

"With growing enthusiasm I poked around down there in the dark chamber. I began to ask questions as to what it was I was 'seeing' down there, and grabbing a pen, began to sketch out the machinery innards. When I actually located the magnetometer itself and described seeing a gold alloy plate there, the impact of observation upon this part of the instrumentation stopped the sine wave altogether."

He managed to keep his attention focused for a full 45 seconds. The moment he "let go," the sine wave returned to normal. His feat produced bedlam among the watching scientists, all of them in turn incredulous at what had happened and wildly inquisitive to know how Ingo Swann had achieved it. Every time he tried to explain, and his attention wandered back inside the squid, the needle of the strip recorder started jumping erratically about as the sine wave frequency again increased.

Dr. Puthoff tried one last time to make sure that what was happening was not coincidence. For several minutes he talked to Ingo Swann about other things, before once more discussing the magnetometer. As soon as this happened, up went the sine wave rate again.

To this day, the experiment remains one of the most convincing demonstrations of psychokinesis on fundamental physical particles. It was written up and presented as a paper to the Conference on Quantum Physics and Parapsychology in Geneva two years later, and Dr. Puthoff's only regret is that, because neither he nor anybody else at SRI expected such an astonishing result, they did not use multiple recording.

"Although Ingo's subjective and mostly accurate description of what the inside of the magnetometer looked like (which he could not have known) provides circumstantial evidence that the effect originated there, we cannot be totally sure that he was not affecting something in the electronics, or in the strip recorder itself."

However, applying the lessons of this research to the Triangle mysteries, it is not all that important to know exactly where the electromagnetic disturbances came about; the crucial point is that here is excellent modern scientific experimentation telling us what had always looked likely from our investigation of the strange and erratic behavior of electronic navigational equipment in ships and planes—it was possible for them to be affected by the human mind. Man-machine interaction was now a proven fact.

One aspect of all Ingo Swann's work is the way that he consciously directs the result. It is his own will to alter the reading on a magnetometer or change the heat in a thermistor, and this is a talent shared by the psychics who can be grouped with him: for example, Nina Kulagina, the Russian woman who has been filmed moving matches and other objects across a table purely by exerting some psychokinetic force that she is able to generate.

Uri Geller, too, has found that some of the effects he produces become easier to attain with practice. Working with the physicist Andrija Puharich, some of the earliest experiments involved Geller's exerting a mental force over a standard "Silva"-type compass laid flat on the table in front of him. At the first attempt it took some seven minutes of concentration before he was able to move the compass needle 16° clockwise.

Dissatisfied by this result, Geller then placed a tourniquet of rubber bands on his left hand. This time, still with a great deal of mental effort, he was able to move the compass needle 90°. After the experiment Geller complained that he had never worked so hard, and suggested it might have been easier had there been a crowd of people nearby from whom he could "draw energy."

By December 1971, Geller had accumulated a great deal more experience, and the experimental results were coming faster and more easily. Andrija Puharich recounts: "We began with Uri testing his power on the Silva compass which was lying on my study table. He placed his hand over the compass and the needle literally spun. He moved his hand away and as we talked about the ease with which he now moved a compass compared to his efforts just one month ago, the compass vanished before our eyes. We searched the entire apartment, and I found the compass lying on the floor of the bathroom."

So far as the Triangle is concerned, there are a number of interesting elements to this part of the Geller story. First, although the compass disorientation *seemed* in the first place to require the expenditure of a great deal of energy, this later turned out not to be the case; as became steadily clearer during our investigation, you do not necessarily have to propose absurdly large amounts of energy to account for the weird eletromagnetic anomalies observed.

Second, this incident provided our first clue that electromagnetic disturbance, indicated by the spinning compass, was somehow linked with disappearance, in the way that the compass simultaneously vanished. True, on this occasion the compass must have disappeared into another dimension only briefly, but it was strongly suggestive evidence.

Third, there is not always cause and effect in these psychokinetic events. Although Swann, Kulagina, and Geller try to "make" something happen, very often it does not happen as they expect it to. Geller did not try to make the compass disappear, and there are many similar examples of unexpected side effects that we also came upon. In other words, whatever this mysterious "fifth force" may be, it has an unpredictable and involuntary nature to it—and can thus be even more strongly suspected of being present in the cabins and cockpits of some unwitting navigators in the Triangle.

Uri Geller, for example, later went to Stanford Research Institute to be examined by Dr. Harold Puthoff and his colleague Dr. Russell Targ. He was trying much the same experiment as Ingo Swann, but on a different type of magnetometer, when the two delicate pens on the strip recorder bent off the chart recorder, with Geller being continuously filmed some distance away. The damage to them was quite severe; red ink was dripping from both twisted pens. But ostensibly, all Geller had been trying to do (successfully) was to alter the magnetic field.

There was, according to the two scientists, "an almost limitless list of equipment failures associated with our attempts to observe Uri's paranormal ability"—and equally, a number of unanticipated events. Filming his efforts to bend some wire rings inside a plastic box, they heard a strange noise coming from inside the movie camera.

"One of the small pulley wheels had disappeared from the film magazine, and four hundred feet of 16mm film was being crammed into the body of the camera, an event our cameraman considered impossible under the conditions for film-loading in use. We have no good explanation for the disappearance of this wheel, although it turned up a day later on the enlarging easel in a neighboring darkroom."

On one of their last days with him, they set up an elegant experiment in which the central purpose was for Geller to deflect a laser beam which was being monitored as usual by a strip chart recorder. Geller said, "Oh, I understand; you want me to move that little pen." He promptly held his fist about two feet over the instrument and shouted, "Move!"

The two scientists reported: "The pen moved all the way across the paper and never moved again. For reasons never determined, the sensitive preamplifiers of both channels of the recorder burned out and had to be replaced."

Since Uri Geller's activities have been subjected to intense scrutiny, and a widespread public suspicion exists that because he is a professional magician, he sometimes uses tricks to help out his psychic functioning, it should be said that our investigation was careful only to consider truly inexplicable cases, such as the ones above. But in any case, the effects of people on magnetism exist outside the Geller phenomenon. In Great Britain, for instance, Suzanne Padfield, married to a top Cambridge physicist, has many times demonstrated her ability to make a compass needle spin inside a sealed glass jar. Professor John Hasted of Birkbeck College in London, whose branching-universe theory was examined later in our investigation, has now experimented with more than a dozen people who can achieve the same result; others have been able to create a nightmare latticework net of jumbled paper clips inside sealed glass globes.

So we can take it that both electromagnetic and electronic machinery, and physical objects, can be grossly distorted in the presence of certain people. We do not know yet whether the person always causes the distortion, for there are often inexplicable side effects. It may therefore be that the fifth force is independent of the person, but needs the person as an agency through which to work—and this is certainly the explanation which nearly all the psychics themselves prefer. It is how it "feels" to them.

In most of the Triangle mysteries that have so far been examined, we can only speculate that these phenomena have been involved; our investigation had been dealing on the whole with incidents long in the past, for which there is today only too little firsthand evidence, and of course many of the people who could have given us the necessary information are now tragically dead.

However, there are a number of reliable witnesses who can give support to these electromagnetic aberrations and who by any standards would be regarded as reliable witnesses. One such is Don Henry, 30 years a seaman, and at the time of the incident in question captain of a marine salvage tug towing a barge from Puerto Rico to Fort Lauderdale on a calm day in 1963.

Don Henry was asleep below when the uncanny disturbance began. In his own words: "I'd been on the bridge for about twenty-four hours. I went back to my cabin to get some sleep, and just as I was nodding off I heard a noise on the bridge, the crew yelling among themselves.

"The only thing I could think of was, oh hell, another fight. So I got up, tore out on the bridge, and asked what was going on, and they told me, 'Cap, everything's going crazy. We've lost the horizon, the compasses are spinning, the gyro's spinning . . . . We just don't know where we're going, we don't know where we are.'

"Now the first thing any captain does the minute he steps on the bridge is that automatically he looks at the compass, and sure enough it was spinning—not fast, but definitely spinning."

What he didn't know at the time was that the electric generators had also stopped temporarily. But even more strange (although closely paralleled by some of the telekinetic disappearances associated with psychics) was what happened next. It was an unnerving experience.

"I went below to the towing deck and grabbed the towing harness to find out what was happening there—like, if there was anything wrong. Not that you could pull it, because of the weight, but if you knew what you were doing you could feel if there was something on the end of it. And there was, definitely. It was taut and tight, just as it should have been with a tow on the end.

"But when I looked, I couldn't see anything. The barge had gone. The line went into the water and then up again through the surface just like it was attached to the barge, but the barge wasn't there. The line seemed to stop. You could see through, right past it, the line sticking up in the air, like a rope trick or something.

"The distance must have been eight to nine hundred feet. In bad weather we had it out to eleven hundred feet, but there was nothing wrong this day, you could see as far as you liked, visibility excellent."

Then, according to Don Henry's account, he went back up to the bridge and ordered full ahead on the engines. He says the throb of the engines picked up and the tug came to life at once—but with no movement forward, as if some immovably fixed object was holding them back. The tug's powerful props, which had successfully pulled the barge behind it through a severe storm and headwind on the previous day, made no impression on this unseen force.

Before Don Henry's eyes, the situation went back to normal.

"The barge came back. I mean, it just materialized. It wasn't like one second it was there and one second it wasn't—it was more gradual than that, like a slow fade in the movies or TV, slow enough for us to watch it happen. And as soon as it got back, the tug just took off like a scalded cat. I slackened off the engines and put a boat over the side to check up if there was anything wrong with the boat or the barge, and there wasn't. The only thing you could find was the tow being warmer than it should have been—not hot, but like it had been twisted or had a lot of energy put through it.

"So we got back on the boat, and I just gave one order—let's get the hell out of here—and we did.

"I checked up with the crew and all the equipment after, and during that time when we couldn't see the barge I reckon every damn thing on the tug had gone dead. Every battery was dead, even flashlight batteries. There was no transmission, no reception on the radios of any kind. I knew myself the radar wasn't working, because I looked to see if it was picking up the barge, even if it was invisible to us, and there was nothing on the screen, nothing. Not even the scanner line was showing.

"As soon as the barge came back into sight again, everything was fine. Except for the flashlight batteries, that is. They were completely useless."

This mention of the flashlight batteries is directly reminiscent of an incident during astronaut Ed Mitchell's association with Uri Geller. At one point during this time, their research was watched by Wernher von Braun, rocket designer for the U.S. space program. After Geller had carried out some metal-bending experiments, von Braun's secretary said that the pocket calculator she was using had ceased to work. The batteries had been checked out as fully charged immediately before the experiment.

Clearly, the discharge had happened at the same time as Geller was employing some kind of energy during the metal-bending. Von Braun wondered whether the energy flow could work in the opposite direction, and he handed Geller the calculator. After the calculator had been in his hands for 30 seconds, von Braun took it back and tested it. The panel lights worked, but the display consisted of random numbers—the circuitry was still not working as a calculator should, perhaps because the batteries were not yet fully charged. Geller held it again for another 30 seconds. After this, von Braun found the calculator worked normally.

Other electromagnetic phenomena have been scientifically recorded concerning Geller's abilities, this time high in the radiative spectrum. Working with Professor John Hasted at Birkbeck College, he was given a geiger counter (which measures X-ray radiation) and asked to hold it to see if the count rate increased. Under normal circumstances, the counter was set to click once or twice a second. With Geller it soon showed a burst of 25 counts per second, later reaching a peak approaching 200 counts—enough radiation, if sustained, to kill. A magnetometer running alongside the geiger counter during the experiment showed simultaneous anomalous bursts. Hasted was left in no doubt that an unusual form of energy was being generated by, or was functioning via, Geller.

Our investigation found another aspect of Uri Geller's career that, shared by some other people with psychokinetic ability, may have a direct bearing on Triangle mysteries—for instance, the persistently reported case of a scheduled airliner en route to Miami during 1971 which disappeared off radar for a full ten minutes. This is, we found, an uncommon but feasible event sometimes happening in certain weather conditions, and certainly none of the passengers were aware that anything untoward had happened when they touched down safely.

Except for one thing. When they landed, all their watches were ten minutes slow.

This concept of a time-slip, which itself is central to any theory that attempts to go beyond Einstein's relativity equations, is mirrored in some of Uri Geller's activities. Early on, with Andrija Puharich, he demonstrated that he was able to stop and start a watch at will. Sometimes the hands bent. At other times they moved, apparently of their own accord, to a time that had previously been suggested by Pucharich.

But more importantly for the purpose of our Triangle investigation, this interference with watches and clocks (which are, after all, only mechanical devices to indicate what is happening at the present moment) seems to transcend time and distance. Puharich's publishing editor in New York, after a brief meeting with Geller, discovered some hours later that an antique watch of hers that had long ceased to work was now functioning perfectly; what was more, it worked without stopping for three and a half days, when its winding mechanism had a maximum of 36 hours. It has gone normally ever since.

On television the results can be even more dramatic. After his first TV appearance with the British interviewer David Dimbleby, a respected reporter for the prestigious *Panorama* program, when viewers saw the hands of a watch bend untouched under the camera's gaze, hundreds of telephone calls were received telling of clocks and watches stopping and starting, and even of falling from mantelpieces and shelves where they had always stood safely—until Geller appeared on TV that night.

An even more spectacular (and better-investigated) case of mass random psychokinesis via TV came when the gifted young British psychic Matthew Manning went on the *Wednesday Special* in Tokyo, a 90-minute program run by NET-TV and set up on this occasion by the well-known psychic researcher Toshiya Nakaoka. Unlike Uri Geller, there has never been the slightest suspicion that the extraordinary psi events that have happened in the life of Matthew Manning are anything but genuine. He is a reserved, totally honest, middle-class doctor's son, whose two books about his experiences (*The Link* and *In the Minds of Millions*) now provide him, in his early twenties, with a living as a writer.

Under no circumstances will he employ his gifts in any form of a stage act—and indeed, like Ingo Swann, he is extremely careful to allow only a few groups of scientists to experiment with him, because of his insistence that all experiments must have foolproof controls.

As a teenager he and his family had been plagued by poltergeist outbreaks in his house. They started in a relatively minor way, with a pewter tankard being mysteriously displaced in the early hours of several mornings, followed by rappings and strange noises. Gradually the objects being moved became larger—tables, wardrobes, bookcases. On one occasion a heavy table was found to have moved through two stories directly from the second floor to the basement beneath, with the various ornaments on top of the table still exactly in position—a clear case of dematerialization and materialization.

At his boarding school the havoc continued, witnessed by his schoolmates in the dormitories and by the teaching and nursing staff. Heavy steel double-bunk beds moved of their own accord. "Apports"—materializing objects—arrived regularly: knives with an ancient royal crest, pebbles, broken glass, nails, skewers, pieces of broken concrete, often apparently flung with such force against the walls that their noise made sleep almost impossible.

Several times his headmaster was on the brink of asking him to leave. Psychic investigators and church leaders were involved.

Then Matthew Manning found a way of controlling the poltergeist phenomena. If he allowed himself to be used for automatic writing or drawing —to let people apparently long dead use him as a medium for their messages or paintings—the poltergeist activities ceased.

If he failed to practice this strange talent, in which he put himself into a mild trance and then produced perfect examples of the work of artists both known and unknown (among those who "signed" were Albrecht Dürer, Rowlandson, Picasso, Leonardo da Vinci, Aubrey Beardsley, and Paul Klee), the poltergeist would remind him of its presence by moving about small objects, "in a mischievous way," he says.

Although the link between automatic writing and the uncontrollable fifth force is evident to

Matthew Manning, our investigation could find no ready connection with anything ever reported in the various Triangle mysteries. However, it became perhaps the best-publicized and best-attested of his activities, since it is a talent that he can switch on more or less at will and which has astounded the world's leading art authorities, none of whom have been able to offer a remotely satisfactory explanation in orthodox terms.

It became relevant to the Triangle because it is also highly visual, and thus suitable for television—and it was this that led to the extraordinary night in March 1976 on Japanese television. Toshiya Nakaoka, after filming a Cambridge, England, to Tokyo telepathic attempt by Matthew Manning with a significant degree of success, asked him if he would fly to Japan to demonstrate automatic drawing, the test being that he would be asked to "make contact" with a Japanese or Chinese artist from the past—by implication, one with whose style Matthew Manning would be completely unfamiliar.

Manning agreed, warning him, "You may have one or two poltergeist effects." A pattern had recently seemed to emerge that whenever he went into television or film studios, there was almost invariably interference with electric or electronic equipment: cameras failed, TV monitors went on the blink, lamps exploded, film was spoiled.

At that stage, however, Matthew Manning had no idea how true his prediction would come. He duly wrote automatically in a temple of mystical Buddhism; the strange brushwork characters that emerged on the page turned out to be in an almost unknown ancient script, Bonji. At another temple he automatically drew some authentic Chinese scenes in a woodblock style, though not in his own view very satisfactorily.

To fill out the program, Nakaoka wanted some more ideas. On a hunch, Matthew Manning suggested a phone-in—he thought that perhaps he could instigate some strange psychokinetic happenings in other people's homes. At most, he said later, he expected "four or five calls."

He took with him to the studio a box full of apports from earlier days at home and at school: a granite-hard 200-year-old bread roll; a fish-shaped snuff box; some beads; a fossilized leaf. The host on the show was somewhat disbelieving. Manning simply told him, "Let's see if anything like it goes on in people's homes tonight, and then you may be convinced."

A couple of minutes later came the first phone call, from a terrified woman who, watching the program with her children, had seen a large glass ashtray in front of the TV set explode noisily into two pieces.

Immediately the studio went berserk, the carefully-planned schedules going by the board. The 25 lines were jammed; some 1,200 calls were received, and several hundred noted and recorded before the telephone fuses blew. Instead of the normal 10 percent viewing figures, the ratings shot up to 27 percent, beating handsomely the previous all-time record (the Muhammad Ali/Japanese wrestler contest with 16 percent). While NET stayed solidly on the air, all five other networks suffered untraceable interference. TV sets switched on—or switched channels—spontaneously, showing his program. Some color TV sets became black-and-white; black-and-white receivers suddenly showed up in full color.

Matthew Manning retained 216 of the most interesting accounts; many of the most important were investigated personally by Toshiya Nakaoka, in order to establish their authenticity. All over Japan that night there was bedlam. Objects materialized—coins, dolls, a long-lost ring. Broken watches started; good watches stopped. Taps turned themselves on. Burglar alarms were set off. Glasses and bottles shattered in front of people's eyes. Car engines started without ignition keys. Boiling water turned to ice. A skeptical journalist, to his chagrin, filmed 150 worth of Japanese yen as they burst spontaneously into flames in his own home.

It was the biggest multi-psychokinetic event the world has ever seen, and Matthew Manning is cautious about giving an explanation for it: "It was difficult to say who was causing these things to happen; the people themselves, or me. They were not with me, as a studio audience is; they were miles away, the length and breadth of Japan. I believe a kind of psychic hysteria was released; reports of phenomena triggering off more phenomena.

"It seems unlikely either that people were fraudulently contriving or that all could have been imagined. I can't see someone burning 10,000 yen notes for fun and mischief. The voices we heard on the program were tearful, frightened, upset. In a way it was as if everyone had been taken unaware, defenselessly. . . ."

His experience may throw light on both contemporary and historical Triangle mysteries. Our investigation tracked down Bob Spielman, a veteran pilot with more than 3,000 hours in the air, much of it over the Bermuda Triangle. In the summer of 1969 he loaned his Beechcraft Bonanza to friends, who crashed it, dying in the accident, some three quarters of a mile inland from the Florida coast. It was a tragedy that might have been put down to lack of experience, or engine failure—except for one inexplicable fact that came up at the FAA/CAB investigation.

The plane itself was relatively intact. But on the shoreline, nearly a mile away from the accident, searchers found one wing of the plane, sheared or wrenched off while the plane was still airborne.

Analysis of the fractured metal could come up with no explanation of how such a giant force could have been applied. Is there a link here with metal-bending and -breaking by people with psychokinetic ability? For in these cases, too, as has been shown by Professor John Taylor and Kings College in the University of London, the molecular disturbance is like nothing produced by the normal forces known to physicists.

Spielman himself is convinced that something unearthly happened on that occasion, and he has another story which suggests that he or his friends may be unwitting agents for fifth-force, or electromagnetic, disturbances. The day after he was filmed for the Bristol-Myers TV show *In Search of the Bermuda Triangle* in 1976, he took off with three friends from the Ocean Reef Club in a twin-engined Piper Comanche, heading for a private airstrip in the Keys. As usual, he checked his instruments before leaving.

"We took off with both tanks three-quarter full. We weren't off the ground 250 feet and my compass started spinning round crazily and—get this—the engine quit. Just quit, like that.

"It put me in a kind of panic, I can tell you. Two hundred fifty feet off ground, couldn't get Miami Approach Control, the wilderness of the Keys underneath.

"I looked at the fuel gauges, and the left and right tanks both read empty. But then the right fuel tank suddenly shot up to one-third full, and I switched power over to that one. Thank God, the engine fired, and we were okay.

"But that compass never worked again, even though they stripped it down afterwards and couldn't find anything wrong with it. And the other weird thing was, something had extracted the fuel from that left tank so completely that there wasn't even any vapor in it."

Could the disappearance at Christmas, 1967, of the cabin cruiser *Witchcraft*, with its ominous-sounding name, fit in the same pattern of demate-rialization? Its owner, hotelier Dan Burack, took it with his friend Father Patrick Horgan to watch the festive lights of Miami. They roared off into the darkness of the night, their powerful search-lights pointing the way; the water was choppy, but not dangerously so. And *Witchcraft* was, after all, virtually unsinkable, with double-shelled hull and sophisticated SOS gear.

Suddenly there was a jolting shudder as the boat hit something underwater. The engines stopped. Dan Burack radioed back to the coast-guard saying what had happened. He gave his exact position, near marker Buoy Seven less than a mile from the coast. The rescuers imagined it would be a routine job to bring the *Witchcraft* back in.

It did not turn out that way. When they arrived at the appointed spot, the cruiser had simply vanished. Not even pieces of the boat were found, though its body was sealed with flotation gel. Nor did a subsequent search covering hundreds of square miles achieve anything better. Not a sign was ever found of the boat or the two men.

The simultaneous disappearance of two KC-135 Stratotankers in August 1963 is another candidate for psychokinetic action.

What is known about the disappearance of the two planes is extremely brief. They left Homestead Base, Florida, on a classified mission over the Atlantic. They sent in routine reports some 300 miles west of Bermuda, and after that there was no contact. Whatever happened must have occurred so quickly that there was no time for an SOS. The unlikely possibility of a mid-air collision between two experienced pilots in good weather turned into an impossibility with the discovery of two patches of debris separated by 160 miles.

This time the psychokinetic explanation would not be dematerialization, because of the wreckage found—and this has always been the puzzle surrounding the crashes: How could they have happened at exactly the same moment? Instead, our investigation felt it was necessary to consider that it might be an example of the unexpected side effect seen so often in tests on Uri Geller and others—the "lightning-striking-twice syndrome," it might be called.

But for the best definite evidence of that form of psychokinesis known as teleportation, our investigation goes back to historic times, to the years between 1812 and 1820 in Barbados. During this time the mausoleum in the Christ Church Graveyard belonging to the wealthy Chase family be-

The Bimini Wall. Is it, as many believe, a remnant of lost Atlantis?

The magnetometer, used for measuring the intensity
of the earth's magnetic field.

A waterspout in Triangle waters.

A victim of the Triangle—Captain Worley aboard the Cyclops
(from the feature film, *Secrets of the Bermuda Triangle*).

The Cyclops

Are such enigmas as Stonehenge and the great pyramids of Egypt and South America related to the Triangle mystery?

Stonehenge

The Gizeh complex

Uxmal—Temple of Magician

Temple of Kukulcan, Chichen Itza

English burial mound

Palenque

From sail to steam, many ships have sunk beneath the Triangle waters. But more mysterious are those that simply vanished without a trace...

Today's Coast Guard uses helicopters as well as cutters to patrol the Triangle.

Carolyn Coscio was flying only 600 feet above a brightly lit hotel—but thought herself lost. She could see only a desert island beneath her...

Carolyn's plane (from the feature film, *Secrets of the Bermuda Triangle*).

A child's body is brought to the Chase vault (from the feature film, *Secrets of the Bermuda triangle*).

The coffin is lowered into the vault.

Heavy lead coffins within the sealed vault were found
tossed about like toys.

Of the many tragedies of the Triangle, perhaps the disappearance of Flight 19, five Avenger planes on a routine training flight, has most captured the imagination of the public.

Eagle Bolliton, who loved to fly, was turned back from this particular mission.

An Avenger (from the feature film, *Secrets of the Bermuda Triangle*).

Boarding an Avenger (from the feature film,
Secrets of the Bermuda Triangle).

For forty-five desperate minutes, Robert Cox, who had just taken off
on another mission, was their only contact with the outside world.

Author Alan Landsburg with radio personality Ray Smithers, whose hot-line show on the Triangle unexpectedly added its own mysterious event to the annals...

came notorious for the eerie happenings that went on inside.

Over the nine years the tomb was opened five times. On each occasion, in spite of increasingly strict precautions to make sure that no unauthorized entry could be made into the tomb, the coffins inside had been moved (or had moved themselves) in a way both inexplicable and macabre. The facts of the case, which became so celebrated in its time that the Chase family grave became the best-known tourist attraction in Barbados, were reported in the May 1945 issue of the *Journal of the Barbados Museum and Historical Society*. In summary, the sequence of events is as follows:

1. On a summer afternoon in 1812, the tiny body of ten-year-old Dorrie Chase was laid to rest beside that of her little sister and an aunt. Hers was a tragic death. She had deliberately starved herself to death—to escape, it was said, the tyranny of her father. Her coffin, like her sister's and those of all the other members of the family who were to be buried in the coming years, was made of lead. Only the aunt's coffin, the first to be placed there, was made of wood.

2. One month later, her father, the Honorable Thomas Chase, died. Graveyard workers who opened the tomb fled in terror from what they saw. Because they were slaves, they were at first disbelieved. However, their story was gruesomely confirmed when the rector of Christ Church, the Reverend Thomas Orderson, himself went into the crypt. He saw what he instantly regarded as sacrilege. The two lead

coffins were turned upside down in opposite corners from their original positions, and the wooden coffin lay on its side against a wall. Although slaves were first suspected, they were evidently too frightened ever to have done this. The coffins were re-arranged; Thomas Chase's coffin, so big it took eight men to carry it, was placed in the center. The 910-pound slab of marble that sealed the entrance to the tomb was carefully replaced.

3.   On September 25, 1816, another infant in the family, Samuel Brewster, died just before his first birthday. The tomb was re-opened, block and tackle on heavy A-frames being needed to lift the marble slab. The Reverend Orderson was this time the first to enter. Again, he was horrified. The coffins were dispersed all over the crypt. Even Thomas Chase's immense lead coffin had been moved all the way across to its opposite wall, where it lay on its side—the work of at least six men, if indeed it was a human force that had moved it. Again, the coffins were replaced and the tomb was sealed. When the A-frame was removed, eight men tried to shift the marble slab in order to test whether it could be budged; it did not shift an inch.

4. Less than two months later, the mausoleum had to be opened again to take the body of the little boy's father, Samuel Brewster, who had been murdered by slaves. On this occasion the Reverend Orderson was accompanied by the Governor of the island, Lord Combermere, and a Justice of the Peace. The usual scene of devastation awaited them. Only the wooden coffin, now crumbling badly, was untouched; the rest

were scattered and upturned in a way that was now becoming eerily familiar. The Governor ordered all the coffins to be removed and a careful check made on whether it was possible to gain entry other than through the front entrance. It wasn't. Once again the coffins were replaced; the marble slab was lowered into position, and this time cemented in place.

5. During the next three years the Chase grave became notorious, with a constant stream of sightseers both from the island and from visiting ships. Ghoulishly, the next burial was awaited with expectancy. It happened on July 7, 1819, after a relative of the family died. Officials examined the cement seal. It was undisturbed. The marble slab was so hard to remove that sledge hammers and wedges had to be used to loosen it. When finally it was lifted, onlookers saw what had caused the difficulty—the great lead coffin of Thomas Chase had been wedged tight against it. Inside, every coffin was out of place (except the wooden one); the three children's coffins were scattered at random, where previously they had been placed carefully one on top of another. This time the vault was submitted to scrutiny by the Royal Engineers. There were no cracks or chips on the inner walls. The ground was probed inch by inch for subterranean vaults or passageways. The crypt was bone dry—not a drip of water had penetrated its thick walls and ceiling. When the coffins were re-interred the position of each was carefully recorded. The floor was covered with fine white sand, which would show up any footprints of intruders. When the marble entrance

block was replaced, official seals were marked in the wet cement seal. It was now impossible for anyone to gain entry without leaving evidence they had done so.

6. Some six months later the Governor decided that, although no death had occurred in the Chase family, he must re-open the tomb in order to quell the growing rumors of voodoo and witchcraft that had grown up around the graveyard. Confident that this time he would find nothing, for the seals on the cement were still unbroken, he had the marble slab removed. He was wrong. This time it seemed as if the coffins had been literally flung about. Men entering the tomb had to climb over the top of the children's caskets. Yet the white sand was completely undisturbed. The Governor, at the same time appalled and baffled, instructed the Chase family to make other arrangements for their burials. The "House of the Living Dead," as one of the newspapers dubbed it, was never used again.

The episode remains one of the best-documented cases of psi in history, and even today there is no way of explaining what happened without having recourse to some kind of psychic or fifth force as demonstrated by the people whose work our investigation had been examining.

So far, we had found that every proposed solution to the Triangle mysteries was leading us, via electromagnetism, to the ideas of another dimension. Men's minds becoming disoriented by magnetic changes; tiny chemical imbalances in the body creating a change of consciousness; fireballs that appeared apparently from nowhere; objects that materialized and dematerialized; poltergeist activity triggered by a force unknown to science—all these things were known to happen in the Triangle.

And all of them fundamentally electromagnetic in nature, for that is how we perceive things on this Earth.

It was time now to go carefully through every disappearance listed in the Triangle literature, one by one, to see just how many might have an extraordinary, rather than a natural, explanation; to find out if the Triangle truly contains more than its fair share of other-worldly occurrences.

It was to be on illuminating experience.

CHAPTER FIVE

The Master List

The list that follows is the most comprehensive ever compiled on the disappearances and anomalous events that have taken place in the Triangle during recorded history. It was drawn up from all the major source books on the subject, from original historical records such as *Lloyd's Register,* and from the new cases that were uncovered by our investigation.

Where no official verdict has gone on public record, we have simply noted the facts of the case. In those events for which there is an official verdict, we considered whether we thought that the inquiry's explanation was, under the circumstances, the most plausible; or whether, in the light of all the new scientific knowledge our investigation had discovered thus far, it was proper to raise queries as to other possible solutions.

In the first instance, we naturally let the verdict stand. However, there was a formidable number of cases where the official explanation seemed both implausible and inadequate, as will be shown. There are, after all, a number of understandable reasons for bias, conscious or unconscious, in an official inquiry. Inquiries have a well-founded desire not to disturb people's peace of mind; at the same time most orthodox scientists or academics are predisposed to reject any idea that does not fit the currently accepted model of the way the universe works (although, as we have seen, this model changes all the time). So it has come about that almost every inquiry blames: (i) "exceptional" weather conditions, as if the Triangle were a constant maelstrom of hurricanes and thunderstorms, which of course it is not; (ii) structural failure, even though the ships and planes had been perfectly safe up to the moment of disappearance; (iii) human error, often ascribed to people who up to that moment had a high reputation for experience and caution.

Of course, in many cases one of these three causes, or a combination of them, is correct; what was revealing was the formidable number of question marks to be put against the rest.

SECTION ONE—SAILING VESSELS

CASE 1. August 1800. USS *Pickering* disappeared on August 20 with a crew of 90 en route to Guadeloupe in the West Indies from New Castle, Delaware.

CASE 2. August 1800. USS *Insurgent* disappeared

in the Bermuda Triangle with 340 men on board.

CASE 3. October 1814. The USS *Wasp* failed to return after a Caribbean voyage. She had a crew of 140.

CASE 4. 1840. The *Rosalie* was found abandoned except for a few starving cats and canaries. She was on a voyage from France to Cuba. Her sails were still set, and she appeared to have been abandoned only few hours before she was discovered. There was no damage to the valuable cargo she had aboard.
Additional information. Rosalie was towed to Nassau for salvage. No trace of a ship called Rosalie in *Lloyd's List.*
Official verdict. Rosalie "never existed."
QUERY: Why deny the existence of an event that was fully authenticated locally? Was there something to hide? Is this another "ghost ship" mystery similar to the Marie Celeste? (See CASE 9.)

CASE 5. October 1824. USS *Wildcat* disappeared on a voyage from Cuba to Tompkin's Island. She had a crew of 14.

CASE 6. March 1813. USS *Grampus* disappeared off St. Augustine with 48 people on board.

CASE 7. April 1854. A schooner, *Bella,* left Rio de Janeiro for Jamaica. The ship never reached its destination—only a longboat was ever found.
Official verdict. The ship capsized. Allegedly it was so overloaded that there was cabin furniture tied onto the decks.
QUERY: Why should the ship have had a successful and safe voyage right up to the time it entered the Bermuda Triangle?

CASE 8. 1855. The *James B. Chester* was found abandoned southwest of the Azores. It was boarded by sailors from the *Marathon*, who found no traces of violence on board. The ship's papers and compass were missing, and equipment in the captain's cabin was strewn about.

Official verdict. No adequate records. Surmised that the ship was hastily abandoned for fear of getting caught in a storm.

QUERY: Why should experienced seamen imagine they were safer in a smaller boat—the opposite to all their training and instinct?

CASE 9. December 1872. The *Marie Celeste* was found abandoned north of the Azores by the British brigantine *Dei Gratia.* The cargo was intact, and there were adequate provisions still on board. There were no signs of violence. One lifeboat was missing, and the main cabin was boarded up.

Additional information. The *Marie Celeste* was found outside the Bermuda Triangle, but as it is a classic mystery of the sea it is relevant to investigations into the Triangle. It may also be seen as part of the series of abandoned ships which provide investigators with evidence of irrational behavior. Explanations put forward include: pirates, hijacking of crew, mutiny, fear of dangerous cargo, presence of "ergot" in the bread leading to collective insanity. The *Marie Celeste* had a known history as a jinx ship.

Official verdict. "The greatest mystery of the sea." The explanation to receive most official credence was that of a mutiny. It was said the crew prearranged a hijack by another ship, but that the plans went awry.

QUERY: Why was cargo left on board? Would we

nowadays have to consider the dimensional explanations?

CASE 10. January 1880. HMS *Atlanta,* a training ship, disappeared en route from Bermuda to Portsmouth, England. It had a crew of 290 cadets and officers. When the *Atlanta* was missed, the Navy organized a thorough search, using six ships from the Channel Fleet. The search continued until May without success. No trace of the ship was ever found.

Additional information. The incident was first reported in the London *Times* (3 April 1880) and a series of articles followed. The weather was recorded as unfavorable at the time.

Official verdict. The official investigation blamed the loss on the failure of leadership from the experienced crew members. The argument was that the ship hit bad weather and the predominantly trainee crew were unable to cope.

QUERY: As with the USS Cyclops, *did the weather conditions have a mental effect on the boy officers? Did disorientation lead to disappearance, in the familiar pattern?*

CASE 11. August 1881. A British ship, the *Ellen Austin,* encountered a schooner west of the Azores; it had been abandoned but was still seaworthy. A small salvage crew from the *Ellen Austin* boarded and headed for St. Johns, Newfoundland, in tow. A fog descended and the ships drifted apart. Several days later the ships came into contact and once more the crew from the *Ellen Austin* found the schooner deserted.

Additional information. Most versions of the story mention that a second boarding party also vanished. (See Chapter Seven.)

COMMENT: *Similar to other Triangle disappearances with no orthodox explanation available.*

CASE 12. 1886. *Lotta,* a Swedish bark bound for Havana from Gotenburg, disappeared north of Haiti.

CASE 13. 1868. A Spanish merchant ship, *Viego,* disappeared on a voyage through the Caribbean area.

CASE 14. 1884. An Italian schooner, *Miramon,* bound for New Orleans, disappeared in the Caribbean area.

CASE 15. October 1902. A German bark, *Freya,* sailing from Manzillo to Chile, was found dismasted, crewless, and lying on her side. The anchor was lying free at the ship's bow. The captain's calendar was turned to October 4, so the disaster must have struck soon after the ship left port. But the winds were known to have been light at the time.

QUERY: *Did a violent earthquake in Mexico at the time of sailing have electromagnetic repercussions on conditions at sea?*

CASE 16. January 1908. A bark, the *Baltimore,* disappeared; it was last heard of at East Hampton Roads, Virginia. Nine people on board.

CASE 17. January 1908. A schooner, *George R. Vreeland,* also last heard of east of Hampton Roads, Virginia, set sail and disappeared. Seven people were on board.

CASE 18. September 1909. A schooner, *George Taulane Jr.,* was last seen on the East Georgia coast before she vanished.

CASE 19. November 1909. Joshua Slocum, a famous round-the-world sailor, was lost along with his boat on a relatively short trip from Miami to the West Indies. Although he was 65 at the time, many contemporary commentators said that Slocum was too experienced and the *Spray* was too good a boat to be defeated by the normal hazards of the sea.

Additional information. Many ingenious explanations were put forward for the disappearance— among them that Slocum deliberately sailed away from his announced destination to escape an unhappy marriage. The myriad explanations themselves indicate an element of mystery about the incident.

Official verdict. That Slocum encountered conditions that were beyond him.

QUERY: Is it possible that his mental tension led to a psychic event such as dematerialization?

CASE 20. December 1909. A schooner, *Martha S. Bement,* disappeared east of Jacksonville, Florida.

CASE 21. December 1909. A schooner, *Maggie S. Hart,* disappeared east of Jacksonville, Florida, with eight people on board.

CASE 22. December 1909. A schooner, *Auburn,* disappeared east of Jacksonville, Florida, with nine people on board.

CASE 23. December 1909. A schooner, *Anna R. Bishop,* was lost east of Jacksonville, Florida. There were seven people on board.

CASE 24. December 1913. A schooner, *George A. Lawry,* was lost east of Jacksonville, Florida. There were six people on board.

CASE 25. January 1914. A schooner, *Benjamin F.*

Poole, disappeared east of Wilmington, North Carolina, with eight people on board.

CASE 26. February 1914. A schooner, *Fitz J. Babson,* vanished east of Jacksonville, Florida, with seven people on board.

CASE 27. April 1915. A schooner, *Maude B. Krum,* disappeared east of St. Andrews, Florida. Seven people were on board.

CASE 28. November 1919. A bark, *Brown Bros,* disappeared east of Savannah, Georgia. She had twelve people on board.

CASE 29. January 1919. A schooner, *Bayard Hopkins,* disappeared east of Norfolk, Virginia. She had six people on board.

CASE 30. February 1920. *Amelia Zeman,* a schooner, disappeared east of Norfolk, Virginia, with nine people on board.

CASE 31. January 1921. A yacht, *Carol A. Deering,* en route from Barbados to Norfolk, Virginia, was found abandoned on Diamond Shoals, Cape Hatteras. The yacht had all its sails set. There had been a crew of twelve on board, but the ship was deserted save for a few cats. The yacht showed no signs of damage, but the lifeboat was missing.

Additional information. Many of the captain's personal possessions were missing; this indicated that the ship was not abandoned in an emergency.

Official verdict. The official investigators suggested piracy or political kidnapping as an explanation for the abandonment. Lloyd's of London surmised that the crew of the *Carol A. Deering* had abandoned the yacht during a storm and were picked up by the SS *Hewitt*. This rescue ship went down later with all hands missing.

QUERY: *Again, why would experienced sailors relinquish the relative safety of a large ship (which after all survived the storm) for a small one? Magnetically induced irrationality and disorientation?*

CASE 32. February 1940. A schooner, *Gloria Coalite*, was found abandoned 200 miles south of Mobile, Alabama. The ship had a crew of nine, and there was no apparent reason for desertion.

Additional information. The U.S. Weather Bureau reported severe disturbance in the Gulf a few days after the *Gloria Coalite* set sail. The deck was a mass of wreckage, and the steering gear was disabled.

Official verdict. Captain Halvorsen of the *Cartigan*, which found the *Coalite*, said he had no doubt that the crew of the *Gloria Coalite* had been thrown overboard.

CASE 33. December 1945. A 72-foot schooner, *Voyager II*, was taken down the intercoastal waters by retired army officer Gifford Hitz and was never seen again. No checkpoints along the waterway ever reported seeing the vessel.

CASE 34. December 1945. A two-masted schooner, *Valmore*, was towed from Morehead City, Carolina, by the *Dunworkin*. The towing ship became disabled and cut the schooner free. Later the *Dunworkin* drifted ashore and was wrecked on the beach. The *Valmore* and its crew were never seen again.

Official verdict. Both ships hit treacherous weather, but the wreck of the *Valmore* was never recovered.

CASE 35. December 1946. A schooner, *City Belle*,

sailing from Nassau to Grand Turk Island, was found deserted 300 miles southeast of Miami. The *City Belle* was found perfectly seaworthy with all its equipment in place—except for the lifeboats. *Additional information.* The *City Belle* was found exactly 74 years after the *Marie Celeste* was found, and exactly one year after the infamous Flight 19 disappearance.

Official verdict. Nassau Guardian (7 December 1946) carried a story that seven survivors were picked up from a shipwreck. The story was not followed up. The Weather Bureau reports heavy winds in the area at the time.

QUERY: Why was it never established that the seven survivors were in fact from the City Belle? *Is the "coincidence" of dates a sign of the space-time equation of psychical physics?*

CASE 36. January 1951. A 65-foot schooner, *Home Sweet Home,* was sailing from Bermuda to Antigua through the Sargasso Sea. The schooner and its crew of seven never reached their destination.

Additional information. There were fierce gales at the time with other ships putting out SOS messages.

Official verdict. Gales capsized the schooner with all hands missing.

CASE 37. September 1953. A yacht, *Connemara IV,* was found abandoned between Bermuda and the Bahamas (400 miles southwest of the Bahamas).

Additional information. The planned route of *Connemara IV* passed through Hurricane Connie with its 125-mph winds. There were two other hurricanes in the area at the time. One curious point is how the shell of the yacht survived three hurricanes.

Official verdict. The yacht encountered one or more hurricanes, and all hands were lost.

QUERY: Why should the yacht survive and the crew disappear? Is this not part of a pattern? (See previous cases.)

CASE 38. July 1956. A schooner, *Bounty*, sailing from Miami, Florida, to Bimini, was lost with a crew of four people.

CASE 39. January 1958. A highly prized yacht, *Revonoc*, disappeared on a 150-mile trip from Key West to Miami. The *Revonoc* was a well-equipped and sturdy vessel with an experienced crew who planned their route to keep as close to the shore as possible. An intensive search found only an empty dinghy belonging to the yacht.

Additional information. The crew included the famous yachtsman Harry Conover, and four others; all were highly safety-conscious.

Official verdict. The *Revonoc* encountered storms that the crew was unable to handle.

QUERY: Is not any one of the alternative solutions to Triangle mysteries in general, listed at the end of Chapter Four, more likely?

CASE 40. April 1961. A ketch, *Calistra III*, sailing from Bahamas to North Carolina, disappeared with a crew of five.

CASE 41. 1962. A schooner, *Windfall*, vanished off the Bermuda Islands.

CASE 42. 1962. A schooner, *Evangeline*, vanished on a trip from Miami, Florida, to the Bahamas.

CASE 43. July 1969. Yachtsman Donald Crowhurst was lost in the Triangle area and his yacht, *Teignmouth Electron,* was found abandoned. No adverse weather conditions had been evident. The London Weather Centre reported: "We have recorded no weather phenomena or gale force conditions which could account for the incidents. You can take it from us that the weather is not to blame."

Additional information. Crowhurst was participating in a round-the-world yacht race at the time. His logbooks contained some false entries, and it was suggested that he committed suicide. Another four incidents occurred in the area within a ten-day period.

Official verdict. Crowhurst committed suicide to avoid the public disgrace of being found to forge log entries.

QUERY: What caused his mind to deteriorate? Climatic/magnetic conditions? (See Chapter Two.)

CASE 44. July 1969. A 20-foot sloop, *Vagabond,* was found abandoned by the Swedish ship, *Golar Frost.* The *Vagabond* was found to be in perfect working order.

Official verdict. Open.

QUERY: Part of the same pattern of abandonment?

CASE 45. July 1969. A 60-foot vessel was found floating bottom up in the Triangle area by the British vessel *Maplebank.*

Official verdict. Left open.

CASE 46. July 1969. A 35-foot yacht was found by the *Cotopaxi.* The abandoned yacht was set on automatic steering. No reason for the abandonment was discovered.

Official verdict. Left open.

QUERY: What is the motive for abandoning a seaworthy yacht? Mental confusion brought on by electromagnetic aberrations?

CASE 47. July 1969. A 36-foot yacht was found bottom up by the British tanker *Helisoma* between Bermuda and the Azores.

Official verdict. Left open.

CASE 49. November 1969. A yacht, *Southern Cross*, vanished; last heard of near Cape May.

CASE 50. March 1973. A yacht, *Defiance*, which was carrying a crew of four, was found abandoned and adrift. Its last position was north of Santo Domingo, but the recovery vessel lost the yacht again. A Navy and Coast Guard search failed to locate the boat again.

Official verdict. Left open.

QUERY: Was there electromagnetic interference with the radio equipment?

CASE 51. April 1974. A 54-foot yacht, *Saba Bank*, was lost on its shakedown cruise in the Caribbean. The yacht was equipped with all the latest safety precautions. It disappeared between Nassau and Miami; no trace was ever found.

Additional information. A professional search by the Coast Guard was launched, together with a thorough search by friends of the lost travellers. A large reward was offered for any information about the loss of the yacht.

Official verdict. Left open, but mentions the possibility that the yacht was hijacked for political purposes.

QUERY: If this unlikely explanation is true, why has the distinctive yacht not subsequently been used and seen?

CASE 52. August 1974. A yacht, *Dutch Treat,* was lost on a voyage from Cat Cay to Miami, Florida. *Official verdict.* Left open.

CASE 53. June 1976. *Meridan,* a sailing vessel, vanished between Bermuda ,and Norfolk, Virginia, with five people on board.
Official verdict. Left open.

CASE 54. June 1975. A ketch disappeared north of Bermuda with five people on board.
Official verdict. Left open.

SECTION TWO—MOTOR VESSELS

CASE 1. March 1910. A Navy tug, USS *Nina,* was lost on a trip from Norfolk, Virginia, to Havana, Cuba. The tug was involved in rescue work and was the first known case of a steamship to vanish in the Bermuda Triangle.

CASE 2. March 1910. A steamship, *Charles W. Parker,* disappeared with a crew of 17. Last known position was east of South Jersey coast.

CASE 3. April 1915. *Bertha L. Basker,* a freighter, disappeared on a voyage from New York to St. Martin. Number of crew not known.

CASE 4. April 1915. A freighter, *Silva,* disappeared on a voyage from New York to Antilles.

CASE 5. March 1917. A freighter, *Timandra,* disappeared in the Triangle. Last known position was east of Norfolk, Virginia.

CASE 6. March 1918. A 19,600-ton U.S. Navy collier, *Cyclops,* sailing from Barbados to Norfolk, Virginia, failed to reach its destination. It carried a crew of 309 people and a cargo of manganese ore. A massive search was organized, but no trace of the ship or crew was ever found. The ship sent out no SOS.

Additional information. There have been many suggested explanations—the ship was hit by mines, torpedoes, or it turned turtle, broke in half, or was a victim of treachery and was handed over to the Germans. The *Cyclops* was the first radio ship to vanish.

Official verdict. After considering all the above possibilities, the inquiry was unable to reach a definite conclusion.

QUERY: (See Chapter One.) *Was the mental disorientation of the ship's captain, Commander Worley, influenced by ionization and magnetic field changes? Was this in turn contributory to a physical state conducive to dematerialization?*

CASE 7. January 1921. A sulphur ship, the *Hewitt,* left Sabine Pass, Texas, but never reached its destination in Boston. The *Hewitt* was last heard of when it radioed another vessel north of Jupiter Island, Florida.

Additional information. One of at least ten ships that disappeared in the Triangle area in the first three months of 1921.

Official verdict. Left open.

QUERY: Sulphur/ball lightning combustion?

CASE 8. February 1921. An Italian steamship, *Monte San Michele,* vanished while sailing from New York to London. It left Portland on February

21 with a cargo of grain for Genoa. It disappeared without trace and did not radio an SOS.

Additional information. Evidence of very bad weather with winds exceeding hurricane level. This incident is only one of a series of losses all in roughly the same area.

Official verdict. The ship was caught in treacherous weather.

CASE 9. February 1921. A British steamer, *Esperanza de Larrinaga*, sailing Norfolk to England, was lost in the Bermuda Triangle area.

CASE 10. February 1921. A British tank steamer, *Ottawa*, departing Port Lobos for Manchester, set off from Norfolk, Virginia, on February 21. It was never seen again, after it had brief communication with the steamer *Darlington Court*. No SOS was sent.

Official verdict. Left open.

QUERY: What happened to the radio system? Electromagnetic interference?

CASE 11. February 1921. A tanker, the *Ottawa*, left New York carrying cargo to Europe, but never reached its destination. No SOS message was sent, and no clues were found to the disappearance.

Official verdict. Left open.

QUERY: Why no SOS message?

CASE 12. 1921. A cargo ship, also from Norway, named *Florino*, was lost on a voyage to Europe from New York. No SOS was sent.

Official verdict. Left open.

QUERY: See previous case.

CASE 13. 1921. A Norwegian cargo ship, *Svartskog*, sailed from New York toward Europe. She

failed to reach her destination. No SOS was sent.
Official verdict. Left open.
QUERY: See previous case.

CASE 14. October 1921. A Russian bark, *Albyan*, sailing from Norfolk, Virginia, failed to reach its destination and was presumed lost at sea. No SOS was sent.
Official verdict. Left open.
QUERY: See previous case.

CASE 15. 1921. A Spanish steamship, *Yute*, of 2,974 tons, cleared port on November 14, 1921. On November 17, *Yute* called for help and gave her position as 240 miles off New Jersey coastline, southeast of Cape May. Government vessels and other ships put out to give assistance, but were unable to find any trace of the ship.
Official verdict. Yute floundered in the storms and the crew perished before the SOS was answered.
QUERY: Is this concentration of ship disappearances in 1921 more than a coincidence? As the weather was typical of any year, would today's satellite magnetometers have detected an increase in radiative or magnetic activity?

CASE 16. April 1925. A Japanese freighter, *Raifuku Maru*, left Boston for Hamburg with a cargo of wheat. It encountered problems a day after sailing and put out a highly disputed SOS signal. No trace was ever found of the ship.
Official verdict. The ship encountered storms, and the crew perished before the SOS was answered.

CASE 17. December 1925. A cargo ship, the *Cotopaxi*, disappeared on a voyage from Charleston, South Carolina, to Havana. No trace was ever found of the ship.

Additional information. Heavy storms were reported on the west coast of Florida at the time of the *Cotopaxi's* disappearance. *The New York Times* described the weather conditions as "phenomenal." *Official verdict.* The ship and the crew were victims of treacherous weather.

CASE 18. March 1926. The *Suddufco* sailed from New Jersey for Los Angeles through the Panama Canal, but she failed to reach her destination—no trace was seen after the ship left New Jersey. The *Suddufco* was carrying a crew of 29 and a mixed cargo of 4,000 tons.

Additional information. New York Times reports heavy storms, but as no SOS was sent, the exact date on which the *Suddufco* was lost cannot be pinpointed. The owners of the ship were said to have been puzzled by the loss of the ship.

Official verdict. The ship went down with all hands in heavy storms.

QUERY: If the existence of the Bermuda Triangle disappearances had been recognized at the time, would there have been such a cursory investigation?

CASE 19. October 1931. A Norwegian freighter, *Stavanger,* was lost with a crew of 45 south of Cat Island, Bahamas. No trace was ever found.

CASE 20. April 1932. A Green schooner, *Embirco,* found a motor boat *John and Mary* abandoned 50 miles south of Bermuda. *John and Mary* was registered in New York

Official verdict. Left open.

CASE 21. August 1935. A boarding party from the *Aztec* found the *La Dahoma* deserted. The boat had suffered some damage but had ample provisions on board and the lifeboats were intact.

Additional information. A complex web of myth and reality surrounds the case of *La Dahoma*. The London Times (10 September 1935) suggested that the *La Dahoma* was just another derelict ship about to sink.

Official verdict. Left open at the time and not subsequently finalized.

CASE 22. March 1938. A freighter, *Anglo Australian*, with a crew of 39, was lost somewhere south of the Azores. The ship radioed "all well" as it passed the Azores on its way west. No trace was ever found of the boat and no SOS was sent.

Official verdict. Left open.

QUERY: Why no SOS?

CASE 23. November 1941. The *Proteus* sailed from the Virgin Islands with a cargo of bauxite. It disappeared without sending an SOS.

Official verdict. The *Proteus* was the victim of a German torpedo attack. There was no positive documentary evidence to substantiate this.

QUERY: Fireball explosion?

CASE 24. December 1941. *Nereus,* sister ship to *Proteus* and *Cyclops,* sailed from the Virgin Islands, but it never reached its destination in Portland. No SOS was sent.

Official verdict. The *Nereus* was another victim of German torpedoes. Again there was no documentary proof of this.

QUERY: Is there something beyond coincidence in three sound ships from the same design yard vanishing without sending an SOS?

CASE 25. 1941. A freighter, *Mahukona,* sent out

an SOS signal from a position 600 miles east of Jacksonville, Florida: "Lowering lifeboats . . . crew abandoning ship." Four rescue vessels sailed toward the *Mahukona*, but no wreckage was sighted nor could any survivors be found.

Official verdict. The weather conditions which forced the crew to abandon ship probably wrecked the lifeboats, too.

CASE 26. November 1942. A passenger ship, *Paulus*, bound for Halifax from the West Indies, was lost without trace. No details of the crew were known.

Official verdict. Possibility of German torpedo attack.

CASE 27. October 1944. A freighter, *Rubicon*, was found by a Navy blimp. The only creature aboard was a Navy dog. The *Rubicon* was in excellent condition except for a missing lifeboat. Personal effects of the crew were still on the ship, but there was no clue as to why no one was on the ship. A broken hawser (mooring cable) was hanging down the side of the boat.

Additional information. There was a hurricane in the Caribbean at the time.

Official verdict. The *Rubicon* was beset by the hurricane and the crew perished in the lifeboats.

QUERY: Why did the crew abandon ship when Havana was 200 miles away? How did the ship (and the dog, and the crew's belongings) survive the hurricane, if indeed that ever hit the ship? Should the mystery, instead, be included among other pointless abandonments?

CASE 28. January 1948. A liberty ship, *Sam Key*, whose last known position was northwest of the

Azores, disappeared. There were 43 people on board.
Official verdict. Left open.

CASE 29. March 1948. The *Evelyn K* was found deserted off the Florida Keys. The boat was owned by jockey Al Snider, who had taken a few friends out for a fishing trip. Apparently the party had left *Evelyn K* to go fishing in a small rowboat. The Coast Guard eventually found the rowboat 60 miles north of Rabbit Key. A massive search was launched for Snider and his missing friends, but the bodies were never found.
Additional information. There were sustained winds of up to 48 mph recorded at the time Snider and his companions went fishing.
Official verdict. High winds hit Snider's rowboat, tossing all the occupants into the sea.
QUERY: Why did the boat remain upright?

CASE 30. April 1948. A vessel called the *Wild Goose* was in tow with four on board. Its last reported position was in the tongue of the Atlantic.
Official verdict. Left open.

CASE 31. January 1949. The *Driftwood,* a fishing boat with five or six on board, was lost between Fort Lauderdale and Bimini.
Official verdict. Left open.

CASE 32. June 1950. A 350-foot freighter, *Sandra,* sailing from Savannah, Georgia, to Puerto Cabilo, Venezuela, was never seen again after she had passed Jacksonville, Florida. No trace of the ship or the crew was ever found, despite a massive search organized with the assistance of a local naval base.
Additional information. Reports of winds of up to

73 mph (near hurricane level). The disappearance of the *Sandra* was one of the earliest incidents to arouse interest in the idea of the Bermuda Triangle. *Official verdict*. The *Sandra* was a victim of heavy winds.

QUERY: *Where did the wreckage go? Is it possible that the climatic conditions that sank the ship were also responsible for a dematerialization event?*

CASE 33. November 1951. The *San Paulo*, a Brazilian cruiser of 20,000 tons, was lost after the tugs that were towing it lost contact with the ship.

Additional information. Two tugs were towing the *San Paulo*, as she was destined for the scrap yard. When the weather deteriorated, one of the tugs released the towing cable. After the storm the remaining cable was found to have been severed and the *San Paulo* was gone.

Official verdict. The *San Paulo* sank during a heavy storm.

COMMENT: *Almost certainly this official finding is correct—but the case still has reminiscent overtones of the experience reported to our investigation by Don Henry.* (See Chapter Four.)

CASE 34. December 1954. A bulk carrier of 3,337 tons, *Southern District*, was lost en route from Port Sulphur, Texas, to Bucksport. The ship was 328 foot long and had a crew of 23, and was last heard of near the Gulf of Mexico. No SOS was sent.

Additional information. The vessel had been plagued by steering problems; three men had walked off the ship before she set sail. The *New York Times* (3 January 1955) surmised that the *Southern District* broke in half in a pounding sea.

Official verdict. The *Southern District* was wrecked in a storm.

CASE 35. February 1963. The *Marine Sulphur Queen*, a 425-foot sulphur-carrier, was lost after having been seen 270 miles west off the Florida coast. A massive search was started, but nothing was found bar the recovery of a few lifejackets and a little debris.

Additional information. Several explanations were put forward—explosion in the cargo tanks, structural failures, etc. The Supreme Court ruled that the vessel was unseaworthy, and claims for damages were settled from 1972 onwards.

Official verdict. The Coast Guard inquiry came to no definite conclusion, further than that it was an industrial accident at sea.

QUERY: Knowing what we do now, should not ball lightning be considered as a cause?

CASE 36. July 1973. A 63-foot charter fishing boat, *Sno' Boy*, was lost in good weather on an 80-mile voyage from Kingston to North East Cay, off Jamaica. There were 40 people on board. The only traces ever found were dispersed patches of debris.

Additional information. The vessel was perilously overloaded (according to *New York Times* reports). Several vessels in the area had been held up by storms. There is some confusion between reports of the incident in *Lloyd's Casualty Reports* and in the *Miami Herald*.

Official verdict. The badly loaded vessel was destroyed along with its crew in heavy storms.

CASE 37. December 1967. Two men went out in the cabin cruiser *Witchcraft* to view the Christmas lights of Florida from a mile out to sea. They radioed back saying the boat hit a submerged object, and it was agreed the Coast Guard would come out to tow them home. When the Coast

Guard arrived, there was no sign of the boat or the men. A massive search was launched which covered from the shore to 130 miles out to sea.

Additional information. As the boat was disabled through the collision, it would have had no power to get out of trouble on the sea. However, it is questionable whether they would have had much trouble as they were so near to the land.

Official verdict. The Coast Guard reached no definite conclusions as to the whereabouts of the *Witchcraft.*

QUERY: Another example of electromagnetic anomalies leading to dematerialization?

CASE 38. November 1966. A 67-foot tug, *Southern Cities,* was towing a loaded barge from Freeport, Texas, to Tuxpan, Mexico. Three days after sailing, the tug sent a routine message stating position as 95 miles south of Texas. Nothing was heard from the tug again. A massive search was launched along the expected route. Eventually the barge was found with no damage done to its cargo, and also some debris from *Southern Cities* was found.

Additional information. There was a thorough checkover of *Southern Cities* in dry dock; it had ample safety/radio equipment, etc. The Coast Guard could not determine the exact cause of the loss; no radio messages were given, and there was no knowledge of bad storms in the area.

Official verdict. The *Southern Cities* broke up in severe weather.

QUERY: Is this not a classic case of bad weather being invoked as a cause even though it is one of the least likely explanations? Why no damage to the cargo? Why no SOS? Isn't an unorthodox theory, such as one involving a fifth dimension, just as probable?

CASE 39. November 1968. A freighter, *Ithica Island,* on a voyage carrying a cargo of grain from Norfolk, Virginia, to Liverpool. There were 29 crew on board.

CASE 40. April 1970. A freighter, the *Milton Latradis,* voyaging from New Orleans to West Africa, was lost with a crew of 30.

CASE 41. October 1971. A 3,339-foot freighter, *El Caribe,* en route from Colombia to the Dominican Republic, was lost with a crew of 28 on board. The final radio message placed her about halfway through her voyage; no distress signal was ever received. A joint search by Colombian, Dominican and U.S. navies failed to reveal any new information about the loss.

Additional information. The Administrator-General in Santo Domingo said the *El Caribe* had suffered severe damage on its last voyage, and he thought it had probably sunk. Newspaper reports suggested the possibility of a political hijacking.

Official verdict. The Coast Guard left their verdict open.

QUERY: Possibility of fireball explosion?

CASE 42. April 1971. *Elizabeth,* a 191-foot paper-carrier, was lost on a voyage from Miami to Venezuela. The last radioed position was in the Windward Passage, between Haiti and Cuba. A search from the Bahamas through to the West Indies failed to reveal any trace of the ship. The failure to find any trace of the ship was particularly disturbing because of the nature of the cargo, which under normal circumstances should have left a trail of evidence.

Official verdict. Left open.

CASE 43. November 1971. A 25-foot fishing vessel, *Lucky Edur*, was found abandoned off the South Jersey coast. The crew of three were all missing. The ten life-preservers were all in their place. A massive search by sea and air was organized, but no trace of the crew was found.

Additional information. The ignition switch on the boat's dashboard was turned on, but there was no gasoline in the motor. Weather conditions were excellent at the time, according to contemporary reports.

Official verdict. Left open, but there was some query about the number of people aboard the boat —there may well have been more than three.

QUERY: Could the men have simply vanished into another dimension? Why were the life-preservers not used if there had been a normal emergency at sea?

CASE 44. February 1972. A 572-foot tanker, *V.A. Fogg*, was lost somewhere south of Galveston on a journey to the Gulf of Mexico. A search was launched after the ship failed to arrive on schedule. Eventually a wreck was found with some of the crew members trapped inside.

Additional information. The reason for the sudden sinking baffled investigators—a legend even grew up that the captain was found dead in his cabin with a cup of coffee in his hand.

Official verdict. Coast Guard inquiry and lawsuits still pending. Unofficial sources surmised that the ship's volatile cargo exploded.

QUERY: Ball lightning? But if so, why did the ship sink so quickly?

CASE 45. March 1973. A 341-foot freighter, *Anita*, carrying coal from Norfolk, Virginia, to Hamburg, was lost en route. No SOS was sent out. A search found a lifebuoy from the *Anita;* this was the only debris recovered from the ship.

Additional information. The *Anita*, although sailing some distance behind its sister ship, the *Norse Variant*, may have encountered the same treacherous weather which was said to have destroyed the latter.

Official verdict. Left open.

QUERY: If an explosion in the coal freight deck was the cause, was there an electromagnetic (i.e., anomalous heat) source?

CASE 46. March 1973. The *Norse Variant*, sister ship to the *Anita,* was lost on a coal run to Hamburg from Norfolk. She encountered winds of up to 85 mph, and the sea was running at 35 to 45 feet high. The crew took to the lifeboats, and an SOS was sent out.

Additional information. After a search, a survivor, Stein Gabrielson, was found bobbing on a life raft. Gabrielson gave an account of the hatchcases being ripped off in the storm and the cargo holds being flooded. Gabrielson could throw no light on the fate of the *Anita.*

Official verdict. Storm damage led to the abandonment of ship—only one of the crew survived.

CASE 47. July 1973. A Haitian refugee ship fleeing Duvalier's dictatorship was lost after travelling in convoy with another refugee ship. The Coast

Guard conducted a search without success.
Official verdict. Left open.

SECTION THREE—MILITARY PLANES

CASE 1. January 1945. A B-25 bomber was lost between Bermuda and the Azores with a crew of nine.
Official verdict. Left open—possibility of enemy attack, but no evidence.

CASE 2. August 1945. A PB4YN disappeared between Miami and Bahamas with a crew of 15.
Official verdict. Left open, although possibility of enemy attack.

CASE 3. December 1945. Five fighter planes and their crews disappeared on Flight 19, a routine training exercise from Fort Lauderdale, Florida. The exercise was designed to follow a triangular flight path; there was an estimated flight time of two hours. Each plane had been preflight-checked and was fully equipped with safety and escape equipment. The weather was excellent. At 3:45 p.m. the flight should have received landing instructions; instead, it radioed to control that it had lost its position. Radio contact became increasingly difficult; by 6:30 the planes had disappeared off the map. Several rescue planes were sent to find the missing planes. One of the rescue planes also disappeared.
Additional information. The idea that the mission was somehow jinxed receives corroboration from the facts; the flight commander's reluctance to fly that day, his failure to wear a watch, and his refusal to change the radio to an emergency channel.

Official verdict. The inquiry reached no positive conclusion.

QUERY: (See Chapter One.) *Mental disorientation followed by dematerialization?*

CASE 4. December 1945. A Martin Mariner, a rescue plane for Flight 19, was lost the same day. It took off at 7:27 p.m. and failed to make its position report at 8:30 p.m. The Mariner did not contact the control tower after that. There were reports of an explosion in the air at about 7:50 p.m.

Additional information. The Martin Mariners were supremely well equipped for rescue work, but had gained a reputation as "flying gas tanks." An explosion in the air was observed by the SS *Gaines Mills* at 7:50 p.m.

Official verdict. There was probably a minor fire on board the plane, and an explosion followed almost immediately.

CASE 5. December 1947. A Superfortress disappeared about 100 miles off Bermuda. The Air Force launched an extensive search but was unable to find a trace of the plane.

Additional information. Official speculation has it that a tremendous current of rising air near a cumulonimbus cloud caused the bomber to disintegrate.

Official verdict. The bomber suffered structural failure and broke up under pressure.

QUERY: What force caused the extreme climatic disturbance?

CASE 6. July 1949. Miami International Airport Flight Controller Carlton Hamilton was guiding a C-46 light plane from Bogota, flown by a pilot known to him. Less than 40 miles from safety, the pilot ceased communication, in spite of repeated attempts to contact him from several radio sources. A search launched within fifteen minutes failed to find any trace.

Additional information. Clear weather, lights of Miami visible.

Official verdict. Left open.

QUERY: (See Chapter Three.) *Is Hamilton right in believing that an occasional and selective electromagnetic disturbance can "knock out" all radio and electronic equipment in the immediate vicinity? Can this lead to dematerialization?*

CASE 7. March 1950. A U.S. Globemaster C124 disappeared north of the Triangle on a flight to Ireland. The London *Times* (30 March 1951) reports the possibility of an explosion after the aircraft carrier *Coral Sea* found the sea littered with wreckage on the estimated flight path of the Globemaster.

Official verdict. Left open because of lack of conclusive evidence.

QUERY: Ball lightning? Psi/poltergeist-related activities?

CASE 8. April 1952. A Navy PBY disappeared east of Jamaica with eight people on board.

Official verdict. Left open.

CASE 9. February 1953. A troop carrier, a York Transport plane, with 39 people on board, disappeared on a routine flight to Jamaica. An SOS was sent but was abruptly ended. A search found no trace of the plane or the crew.

Official verdict. Bad weather made a crash into the gale-whipped ocean a strong possibility, but there was no conclusive proof.

QUERY: Were interrupted radio signals a sign of unorthodox energies involved?

CASE 10. October 1954. A U.S. Navy Constellation left Maryland for the Azores with 40 people on board, but it never reached its destination. It carried two radio transmitters, but neither of them was used to send an SOS. A massive search with 200 planes failed to find any clues to the incident. *Official verdict.* No agreed explanation.

QUERY: Was it taken into account that the 40 people on board were trained personnel, some of whom in ordinary flying emergencies would have automatically operated the distress procedure?

CASE 11. April 1956. A converted B-25 was lost in the southeast section of the tongue of the Atlantic. It was a cargo-carrying plane, and there were three people on board. No SOS was sent. *Official verdict.* Left open.

CASE 12. November 1956. A U.S. Navy P-5, a Martin Mariner patrol seaplane, was lost while on patrol in Bermuda with a crew of ten. No SOS call was made, and a thorough search failed to find any clues.

Additional information. A Liberian cargo ship reported seeing an explosion in the area at about 9:00. There was also a report of a life raft being found, but no plane wreckage was ever seen.

Official verdict. Left open because of the lack of irrefutable reports.

QUERY: Should the unreliability of conflicting eyewitness reports evidenced here be taken into account in other cases?

CASE 13. January 1962. A KB-50 with a crew of eight encountered trouble on a trip from Langley

Air Force base to the Azores. It sent a weak SOS, then faded into silence. A six-day search was launched, but no trace of the plane or the crew was ever found.

Additional information. The weather was considered good according to *New York Times* reports, but the search was hampered by poor visibility.

Official verdict. Left open.

QUERY: Was this another example of the "fog" banks, presumably induced electromagnetically, occurring in the Bermuda Triangle?

CASE 14. August 1963. Two KC-135 Stratotankers left Homestead Air Force Base, Florida, on a classified mission over the Atlantic Ocean. The jets had a cruising speed of 600 mph; they made routine reports 300 miles west of Bermuda, and after that there was no contact. A search found debris from a KC-135. But no further clues were found.

Additional information. Two days after the original search, some more debris was found. There was some dispute as to whether this was from a KC-135. This second pile of debris was found 160 miles away from the original pile of debris which pointed to the amazing coincidence of two jets crashing separately many miles apart. The more popular explanation of a mid-air collision involving the two jets solves the tricky problem of accounting for two separate crashes.

Official verdict. Left open, but favored the idea of a mid-air collision.

QUERY: (See Chapters Four and Seven.) *Coincidence/quantum interconnectedness leading to a psychokinetic disaster?*

CASE 15. September 1963. A C132 Cargomaster with a crew of ten disappeared between Delaware and its destination in the Azores. The last message from the pilot indicated that all was well as he gave his position as about 80 miles southeast of the Jersey coast. This was the last message ever heard from the plane. An intensive search was organized by the Coast Guard and Navy planes, but nothing was ever found. High winds and rough seas plagued the search.

Official verdict. Left open, but weather was considered an important factor.

CASE 16. June 1965. A C119 Flying Boxcar left Milwaukee, Wisconsin, to fly equipment out to the base on Grand Turk Island. There was a crew of ten. At 9:15 the pilot reported his position as just north of the Bahamas; after that the plane apparently disappeared. A search was launched and "wreckage" was found from a C119 Boxcar (e.g., chocks, etc.).

Additional information. The "wreckage" did not aid any conjectures because it was all equipment that could have fallen out of the plane without necessarily being caused by a disaster or an explosion. Structural or engine failure was also considered, but there was no radio message which even hinted at problems. The weather was fair at the time. There was also speculation the C119 had been captured by a UFO; Gemini IV was in orbit at the same time and reported a UFO seen over the Caribbean—the Air Force has not yet been able to explain the object which showed up on film as a large white spot on a black background.

Official verdict. Structural failure caused the plane to break up.

QUERY: In the light of modern knowledge of psi phenomena, should not the "ghost" images be given more weight in a poltergeist/psychokinetic explanation?

CASE 17. September 1971. Captain John Romero and his co-pilot left Homestead Air Base, Florida, in a Phantom II F4 jet. Radar tracked the jet to a position southeast of Miami, when it went off the screen. A massive air search was launched with the forces and the Coast Guard, but no trace was found of the missing jet.

Official verdict. Left open.

QUERY: Another of the Triangle's electromagnetic blank spots leading to normal communication being disrupted?

CASE 18. November 1973. Martin Mariner PBM was lost 150 miles south of Norfolk, Virginia. It carried a crew of 19 people.

Official verdict. Left open.

CASE 19. March 1975. A Lockheed Lodestar, last seen between Grand Cayman and Fort Lauderdale, Florida, disappeared. The aircraft carried a crew of four.

Official verdict. Left open.

SECTION FOUR—LIGHT AIRCRAFT

CASE 1. June 1931. *Curtiss Robin,* a high-winged monoplane (2-seater), was lost off Palm Beach, Florida. Herbie Pond had taken the plane on a bootlegging run to Florida. After he made his delivery, he took off and was never seen again. Herbie Pond, one of the most experienced pilots in the business, was the first known aviator to disappear in the Triangle.

Official verdict. Left open.

CASE 2. December 1935. A Wright Whirlwind on a flight from Havana to the Isle of Pines never reached its destination. The crew comprised three Cubans, among them an experienced navigator, and their journey was only 100 miles over very shallow waters. A massive search was organized, but no trace of the plane was ever found.

Official verdict. Left open.

QUERY: Nowadays, would we not look for magnetically induced pilot disorientation?

CASE 3. December 1966. A Piper Cherokee disappeared with two people on board on a flight between Bimini and Miami.

Official verdict. Left open.

CASE 4. January 1967. A Chase YC-122 cargo plane disappeared on a very short flight from Fort Lauderdale to Bimini. A search operation found only an oil slick and some debris thought to belong to the plane.

Official verdict. Left open.

CASE 5. January 1967. Philip Quigley disappeared in his light plane on a journey from Cozumel to Honduras. He had filed a flight plan. Because of international clearance problems, Quigley's disappearance was not realized for four days.

Additional information. Some investigators have suggested this disappearance is one of a linked series occurring during a *"black week."* Quigley and his plane disappeared on the same day as the Chase YC-122.

Official verdict. Not found because of delay in starting search.

QUERY: Was there a collective mental disorientation around that time, brought about by climatic/magnetic field changes, that led to confusion both in the air and on the ground?

CASE 6. January 1967. A Beechcraft Bonanza disappeared after takeoff from Miami. A search was organized, but no trace was found.

Additional information. Robert van Westenborg, a very experienced and safety-conscious pilot, failed for the first time to file a flight plan. The search was delayed, with a consequent lack of evidence, so the mystery remains of an experienced pilot disappearing on a short and familiar journey in good weather.

Official verdict. Left open.

COMMENT: (See Chapter Three.) *The pilot's muddled behavior lends some credence to the query in the previous case.*

CASE 7. January 1967. A Piper Apache disappeared on a trip from San Juan to the Virgin Islands with three on board over a 40-mile stretch of water. A seven-day search by 40 military and civilian planes failed to reveal any trace of the plane, pilot John O. Walston, or the two passengers.

Additional information. For the first time ever, Walston failed to file a flight plan.

Official verdict. Engine failure.

QUERY: Why no wreckage? Why no consideration of the similar pattern emerging in the previous two cases?

CASE 8. March 1969. A two-engined Beechcraft was lost with two doctors on board on a flight from Jamaica to Nassau. It gave an urgent distress call, then contact was lost. Search party covered 50,000 square miles in five days but could not find any wreckage from the Beechcraft.

Additional information. Wrecked fuselage of *another* plane discovered on an island en route, but this plane was never identified.

Official verdict. Left open.

QUERY: (See Chapter Seven.) *Some theories of other dimensions suggest that materialization and dematerialization have to balance. Can this have happened here?*

CASE 9. June 1969. A Cessna 172, piloted by Caroline Coscio, was lost in the vicinity of Grand Turk Island, Bahamas, with one passenger.

Additional information. The pilot was unable to recognize island beneath her and gave confused radio signals.

Official verdict. Left open.

COMMENT: (See Chapter Three.) *A classic case of magnetically induced disorientation.*

CASE 10. September 1969. Mr. and Mrs. Hector Guzman disappeared on their return from Fort Lauderdale to Puerto Rico in a twin-engined plane, fully equipped with lifejackets and rafts. After re-fuelling at Great Inagua Island, they were never seen again.

Additional information. No SOS sent.

Official verdict. Left open.

QUERY: *Does lack of SOS message once again have electromagnetic significance?*

CASE 11. November 1970. Piper Comanche owned

by Orlando Flying Service missing from West Palm Beach Airport en route to Jamaica. Last heard from after 31 minutes. Enough fuel for six hours, estimated flight time four hours. No flight plan filed.

Official verdict. Engine trouble led to crash; search not started until after dark.

QUERY: The same pattern as other disappearances?

CASE 12. July 1971. Two couples in plane owned by Horizon Hunters Flying Club of Miami radioed abruptly that they were ditching in the sea off Barbados. Coast Guard searched 82,000 square miles without finding wreckage.

Official verdict. Left open.

QUERY: What happened so suddenly that the pilot was unable to give a description over the radio? Was it something other than a "normal" emergency?

CASE 13. August 1972. Beechcraft Bonanza rented to two friends of veteran pilot Bob Spielman crashed three quarters of a mile inland from Florida coast. One wing found separately on beach.

Official verdict. (From FAA/CAB report) "No known force" could have wrenched the wing from the plane in such a way as it happened.

QUERY: (See Chapter Four.) Is this linked with the force used in psychokinetic metal-bending?

CASE 14. May 1973. A Navion 16 (low-winged single-engined plane) disappeared between Freeport and West Palm Beach, Florida. The plane, which had two people on board, had radioed the Freeport control tower its destination, but then went out of contact. An FAA and Coast Guard search found no trace of it.

Additional information. Winds were 12 knots, and seas were less than three feet. There were scattered thunderstorms, but the plane could have avoided them.

Official verdict. Left open.

QUERY: Did the magnetic field changes associated with thunderstorms cause disorientation and radio blackout?

CASE 15. August 1973. A Beechcraft Bonanza disappeared on a holiday flight from Fort Lauderdale to Bahamas. The plane was last heard of after getting clearance from Fort Lauderdale. No SOS was sent.

Additional information. Some other planes had attempted to fly to Bahamas at the same time, but had turned back because of the winds and radio interference.

Official verdict. Left open.

QUERY: See previous case.

CASE 16. December 1973. A Lake Amphibian disappeared on flight from Nassau to Fort Lauderdale with two people on board.

Official verdict. Left open.

QUERY: Is it not more than coincidence that at least once a year an almost identical pattern of disappearance emerges?

CASE 17. July 1974. A Cherokee 6 disappeared on a flight from West Palm Beach, Florida, to Bahamas. There were six people on board.

Official verdict Left open.

QUERY: See previous case.

CASE 18. August 1975. A Twin Beechcraft disappeared after it reported its position as west of Great Inagua, Bahamas. There were three people on board.
Official verdict. Left open.
QUERY: See previous case.

SECTION FIVE—COMMERCIAL PASSENGER PLANES

CASE 1. January 1948. A Star Tiger Tudor IV carrying 37 people disappeared between Bermuda and Havana. The plane, owned and operated by British South American Airways, radioed Bermuda to give a position report and state that all was well. That was the last message heard from the plane. A massive search was launched, but was hampered by adverse weather conditions. No trace of the plane or crew was ever found.
Additional information. Three passenger aircraft all operated by British South American Airways were lost in the period January 1948 to January 1949. All the aircraft were in the Tudor IV series.
Official verdict. "No more baffling problem has ever been presented for investigation." No acceptable explanation.
QUERY: (See Chapter Three.) *Magnetic man/ machine effect?*

CASE 2. December 1948. A DC3A charter plane with 30 people on board disappeared on a flight from Puerto Rico to Miami. The last radio message sent estimated the position to be "in sight of Miami." A search was sent out within three and a half hours of the last message being sent. No trace was ever found of the plane or its passengers.

Additional information. The DC3 had a remarkably high record for reliability and safety. It was equipped with the latest safety features for the model. The plane had enough fuel to fly for one and a quarter hours after it had radioed it was approaching Miami.

Official verdict. It lacked sufficient evidence to assign a probable explanation. Perhaps the plane was blown off course and lost radio contact.

QUERY: (See Chapter Three.) *Could an electromagnetic anomaly have led to instrument or radio failure or both? Why was its pilot, Captain Lingurst, so far adrift with his navigation?*

CASE 3. January 1949. A Star Ariel Tudor IV aircraft disappeared between Bermuda and Jamaica with seven crew and 13 passengers on board. After a radioed report to Bermuda saying the flight was on time and giving the expected time of arrival, the Star Ariel was never seen again. A thorough Navy and Coast Guard search started the following day. No trace of the plane or passengers was found.

Additional information. The disppearance happened almost a year after the Star Tiger disappearance. The plane was also owned by British South American Airways, and its circumstances of disappearance were similar to the other case. The third plane owned by British South American Airways to go down was the Star Dust travelling on the London–Santiago route in August 1947. It radioed its destination in Chile only four minutes before expected time of arrival.

Official verdict. Left open. Meteorological report

states conditions presented no complications for the flight. The search started late because of a radio mix-up; no evidence was found during the search.

QUERY: Were the British South American Airways Tudor IV planes in some way psychically doomed? Is it more than coincidence that each time their radios were knocked out?

CASE 4.   June 1950. A DC3 aircraft carrying a missionary contingent to Venezuela disappeared after making a fuel stop at Kingston, Jamaica. A week passed before the plane was reported as being overdue. No record of a thorough search being organized.

Additional information. The flight originated in California and had a 24-hour stopover at Miami. The plane had an excellent flight record.

Official verdict. Left open. Speculation about weather, etc. No surprise about being unable to survive in the sea for a week.

QUERY: Did the crew and passengers meet the same fate as the other passenger planes lost in the Triangle? Is that fate related in a synchronistic way to the other disasters in the period?

SECTION SIX—MISCELLANEOUS DISAPPEARANCES

CASE 1.   October 1965. George Boston was delivering *El Gato*, a 45-foot catamaran-type houseboat from Fort Lauderdale to the Great Inagua Islands The boat stopped off at Great Exuma Islands. Neither Boston nor the boat was ever seen again after he left Great Exuma. The Coast Guard launched an extensive search, but no trace was ever found.

Additional information. Boston was a very experienced sailor, and the route he followed stayed close to land with short hops from island to island.

Official verdict. The *El Gato* had some mechanical problems which Boston rectified before leaving Nassau. They may have recurred, leaving Boston stranded.

QUERY: Why has there never been a plausible reason for Boston to remain stranded?

CASE 2.   May 1968. A nuclear submarine, USS *Scorpion*, with 99 people on board, disappeared on a voyage from the Mediterranean to its base in Norfolk, Virginia. Her last reported position was west of the Azores. No sign was found of the submarine until five months later when a research ship located and photographed a shattered wreck 400 miles southwest of the Azores in 10,000 feet of water.

Additional information. There was no evidence of foul play or of explosions of nuclear power plant or torpedoes. There are several other reports of submarines in the west Atlantic, just outside the Bermuda Triangle.

Official verdict. The Court of Inquiry could come to no positive conclusion. It was suggested the *Scorpion* may have suffered the same fate as the SS *Greenland*, which dived below its maximum depth. However, the crew of the SS *Greenland* noticed the mistake and rectified it just in time.

CASE 3.   August 1969. Two lighthouse keepers, Ivan Major and William Mollings, disappeared from the lighthouse at Great Isaacs Rock. No trace of the two men was ever found.

Additional information. Great Isaacs Lighthouse has a history of supernatural occurrences. There is the legend of the Gray Lady who periodically "walks" the rocks weeping for her child who survived an ancient shipwreck. A Miami fisherman, Bruce Mounier, claims that shortly after the incident of the lost lighthouse keepers he saw two underwater UFOs near the lighthouse. They were moving at high speed just below the surface, he said.

Official verdict. The area is renowned for its treacherous conditions. It seems probable that both men were washed away by the sea.

QUERY: Why should both men—or even one—be washed away, when they had spent their entire careers in such conditions? Is the "ghost" history of the lighthouse a significant factor?

CASE 4. 1953-1974. Disappearance of numerous scuba divers during this period has been noted by various investigators, notably Richard Winer.

Official verdict. Underwater sport is dangerous, and it is only to be expected that there will be occasional casualties.

QUERY: Is the concentration of fatalities higher in the Bermuda Triangle than elsewhere?

CHAPTER SIX

Ancient Knowledge

To most people in the 20th century, the idea of other dimensions and other kinds of consciousness is still difficult to accept. For at least 600 years, Western civilization has been taught to think that only what can be seen and felt and measured is real; anything else is "imagination," or "wishful thinking."

Yet there is evidence that this was not always so. In ancient times, particularly perhaps in times before reading and writing became the essential tools of thought and learning, it is possible that entire civilizations were based on different concepts: they believed that what we observe is transitory, and that alongside us other undiscovered worlds exist where different energies play their part, and which sometimes spill over into the world of our own.

Our investigation led to the decision to look for any vestiges of this long-forgotten knowledge insofar as it might relate to the strange energies and magnetic anomalies in the Triangle. There were three likely candidates in prehistory: the societies that during a period of 2,000-plus years erected the megaliths of northwest Europe, culminating in Stonehenge; the priesthood that understood the secrets of the astronomy and mathematics of the Great Pyramid; and the unquenchable myth of Atlantis, now perhaps at last discovered in part in the physical reality of the underwater ruins at Bimini.

The first two of these societies, it seemed from initial research, may have been deeply absorbed by a study of what we now call electromagnetic forces; similar legends were attached to Atlantis.

And each, it turned out, might be linked more closely in an ancient scientific understanding than anyone had yet suspected.

The clue that the activities of the megalith-builders might be connected to the odd behavior of electric and electronic equipment in the Triangle came from recent research into the magnetic fields surrounding the standing stones and stone circles that cover a 1,000-mile swath on the Atlantic coast of Europe, from Portugal in the south to the Hebrides and Orkney islands to the north of Scotland.

These rough stone monuments have always been an enigma. They are the oldest stone monuments in the world, dating in some cases from 6000 B.C. (for comparison, writing was not used until the time of the first Sumerian civilization, beginning in 3000 B.C., and the Great Pyramid was built around 2500 B.C.). Many of them are 15 or 20 feet in height, and the tallest, the Grand Menhir Brise at Locmariaquer in Brittany, northern France, once stood 57 feet high and weighed 340 tons; an earthquake or similar disaster has felled it, and it now lies broken in four pieces, a mute reminder of the gigantic strength and technique that was once needed to erect it.

There are many puzzles about these stones. Why did a peasant people, who were almost certainly illiterate, devote so much of their energy to hewing and lifting these great pieces of rock? Why were some of the stones—the bluestones at Stonehenge, for instance—quarried up to 150 miles away from the site?

Were the stones placed at random, or in specially chosen locations? Did the stones have anything other than a ritual function?

For many years the orthodox scientific establishment was reluctant to accept that the stones had anything significant to offer a student of prehistory. When excavated (the normal archaelogical method, limiting though it is, of trying to establish the facts of what was going on in a certain past age), the stones had little to offer; burial and/or cremation is sometimes associated with them, but usually there is nothing beneath but earth or bedrock.

It has taken some remarkable detective work, by a handful of people working independently from different standpoints, to show that these stones may not be just the oldest monuments in the world, but also some of the most remarkable. What has recently been discovered about them has profound implications not just for prehistory, but for certain aspects of geology and physics as well; it is this latter aspect that throws light on the magnetic anomalies of the Triangle.

The core of new insight stems from the newly proven fact that the megalith-builders were obsessed with astronomy, and the movement of the sun and moon in particular. Careful surveys of the 900 stone circles that are mostly situated in the British Isles have shown that each one was primarily designed as an astronomical observatory. It has, of course, been suspected since the end of the last century that Stonehenge could be used for this purpose, but not until the recent work by the Scots Professor Thom has it been realized that all the other, usually much earlier, circles had the same function.

We now have to recognize that these early people, without the help of writing as a memory aid or for instruction, were nevertheless able to work out not just the significant times of the year when sunrise and sunset were at their extremes (or equal, at the time of the equinoxes), but were able to do the same for the much more complex movements of the moon, and thus predict its eclipses.

They were able to detect what in astronomical terms is known as the "minor standstill," a phenomenon caused by the moon's elliptical orbit which can only be observed once every 9.3 years. To have come up with the standards of accuracy which we now know megalithic man achieved, these people, five thousand years ago or more, must have spent tens of generations perfecting their knowledge and passing it on by word of mouth alone—presumably through some kind of early priesthood, or, as the leading British astronomer Sir Fred Hoyle suggested, a "university" into which the brightest youngsters were brought from far and wide.

All this is revolutionary thinking compared with the previous picture of primitive man which the textbooks have passed down to us, and it has led to an even more startling proposal: What if this astronomical aptitude was deliberately aimed at releasing the kind of earth forces that still seem to be operating today in the Triangle in a manner which we do not any longer know how to control?

Again, the breakthrough came from dowsers, noted earlier in our investigation as having a special sensitivity in the way they are able to detect weak changes in magnetic fields. They had long said that the standing stones and stone circles contained a lost form of energy, which was activated and liberated at certain times of the year, for instance, the special feast days of midsummer day, midwinter day, and the equinoxes of May Day and November Day.

These dowsers said the power in the stones was energized on these occasions because in some way the position of the sun, moon, and planets had an effect on energy that came up from underground; and this was why the ancient builders of the megaliths were so obsessed with astronomy—they had to know exactly the time when the heavenly bodies would be in the right position for the power to be "switched on."

Now this finding (or rather, belief) is uncannily similar—indeed, almost identical—to what the veteran air traffic controller Carlton Hamilton believes is the cause of the Triangle disappearances. (It was Carlton Hamilton, one of our most experienced witnesses, who had told us the strange story of his pilot friend who disappeared from radio contact less than 40 miles from Miami and was never heard from again, despite a search being launched within 15 minutes.)

These are his own words, as recorded by our investigation: "My belief is that the aircraft, like many others, experienced total navigational failure. I believe that this was caused by some type of condition that exists from time to time in the so-called Devil's Triangle, wherein the navigational equipment of boats and aircrafts is totally disrupted.

"I think that this comes mostly from some type of possible mineral deposits under the water, along with the rotation of the earth, and atmospheric conditions at the time. I believe that it exists only for short periods of time, and only up to an altitude of around 10,000 feet."

The three factors he mentions as causes for Triangle disasters are closely paralled by what dowsers believe about the standing stones. For his underwater mineral deposits read "underground energy created by streams"; for rotation of the Earth read "disposition of the Earth toward the heavenly bodies"; for atmospheric conditions at the time read "special occasions when the power was harnessed." What this veteran Triangle observer says is happening in the Triangle now is in essence the same as dowsers think was happening in the time of the megalith-builders thousands of years ago.

Morover, there is now scientific backing for the dowsers' belief. Francis Hitching, whose investigation of dowsing was described in Chapter Three, enlisted the help of Professor John Taylor, of Kings College University of London, to see if this supposed power could in any way be identified or measured today.

Professor Taylor is a mathematician and physicist of high repute who has studied in depth the metal-bending abilities of Uri Geller and others and has written a definitive popular account of black holes, that strange condition of physics that occurs when stars and galaxies collapse upon themselves and all normal realities become distorted and reversed. On this occasion, he suggested that magnetism, one of the two components of electromagnetism, might be involved.

The experiment was described in an hour-long TV special based on another of Francis Hitching's books, *Earth Magic* (William Morrow/Pocketbooks). It showed a sensitive magnetometer on a wooden hoist being taken up and down the face of a 14-foot standing stone several times.

On each occasion, to the evident astonishment of both Taylor and Hitching, the difference in magnetic field strength between the bottom and top of the stone was enough to push the magnetometer off the scale.

The stone, which should have had no effect whatsoever, was producing a magnetic anomaly no less than one-fiftieth of the strength of the magnetic field created by the entire Earth.

While it took an experienced dowser to recognize this magnetic anomaly, the experiment proved at least two things:

(i) A force strong enough to create the spontaneous distortion effect noted in the Triangle and in other places because of barometric/magnetic disturbances was being generated within the stone in a way previously unrecognized by science.

(ii) It was overwhelmingly likely that the ancient people who put the stones there knew more about this force than we do today—perhaps were even able to control it, so that it became life-enhancing.

Two big, so far unanswered questions are how this knowledge developed, and when and how it was lost. In asnwer to the first, an increasing number of researchers of the megalithic period are looking to the possibility that Plato's Atlantis was indeed a reality, and that the massive underwater stone blocks at Bimini off the Bermuda coast can be seen as part of its remains. These researchers suggest that after the destruction of Atlantis, a handful of survivors sailed across the ocean and settled on the western Atlantic seaboard; they brought with them a somewhat incomplete knowledge of the energies on which the fabled continent has been based, and tried to harness these again with the aid of the local building material, which happened to be the quartz and granite of the area.

Radiocarbon dates support this idea of an easterly transmission of knowledge. All the oldest stone monuments so far discovered are on the coastline of northwest Ireland and Scotland, and southern Portugal, and the dates get progressively younger as they move inland through the British Isles and Europe. The way that farming spread offers a similar indication; radiocarbon dates show a consistent pattern of it developing first in the Near East and Egypt, and then moving outwards from there at a consistent rate averaging one kilometer a year, *with the exception of the lands occupied by the megalith-builders.* Here it developed "spontaneously," according to orthodox modern archaeological theory; but there is equal justification for arguing that it was introduced from the West by a new race of people, such as Atlanteans.

Most of what we can surmise about the civilization of Atlantis comes from the psychic readings of Edgar Cayce, the "sleeping prophet." In the light of our new proof of the reality of psychic events, discussed in Chapter Four, our investigation felt his career and his insights must not be dismissed lightly. Not only did he have a proven track record of telepathic and predictive success, but his thoughts about the nature of Atlantis, outrageous when he first offered them, have become steadily more respectable and plausible in scientific terms.

Like many dowsers, Edgar Cayce believed his knowledge came from another dimension, in which some form of universal mind operated (an idea equivalent to the Eastern idea of Cosmic Consciousness whereby an individual would inherit memories of ancient wisdom in much the same way as an individual inherits the physical characteristics of the parents). Cayce had a profound belief in the reality of reincarnation; he believed that it was possible to make use of past knowledge, obtained psychically, to understand the future.

To tune into this knowledge, he would go into an unconscious trance; in this state, Cayce made diagnoses and prescribed treatments during his career for thousands of individuals and their ailments. Although this practice was greeted with widespread skepticism at first, a homeopathic doctor, Wesley Ketchum, M.D., has testified to Cayce's medical ability:

"I have used him in about 100 cases and to date have never known of any errors in diagnosis, except in two cases where he described a child in each case by the same name and who resided in the same house as the one wanted. He simply described the wrong person. . . .

"The cases I have used him in have, in the main, been the rounds before coming to my attention, and in six important cases which have been diagnosed as strictly surgical he stated that no such condition existed, and outlined treatment which was followed with gratifying results in every case."

When Cayce ventured into world prophecy his "readings" encountered far more hostility—there was no immediate proof of their veracity, unlike the medical readings. However, there was no accounting for the way that on those occasions he would speak ancient Romance languages, even breaking into Homeric Greek on one occasion. His supporters maintained he made incredibly accurate predictions—for instance, that he foresaw two world wars, naming the dates of both; and that he foretold the worldwide financial depression of 1929, describing the stock market crash in detail, and giving the date (1933) when the Depression would come to life in America.

So far as Atlantis is concerned, Cayce insisted throughout that its location was centered in the region now known as the Sargasso Sea and that archaeologists would confirm this at Bimini; his actual words predicting this in 1940 were: "Poseidia will be among the first portions of Atlantis to rise again—expect it in '68, and '69, not far away."

Duly, in 1968, the disputed walls/roads/platforms of Bimini were first seen by a number of divers and fishermen, presumably after they had been uncovered by geological movement. According to orthodox academic opinion, these stone blocks are natural rocks smoothed down after centuries of erosion; but nobody has been able to explain the regularity of their formation, and an alternative explanation is more likely.

Certainly the region has a history of topographic disturbance and geological turmoil which is not inconsistent with the "dramatic sinking" of Atlantis more than 10,000 years ago. Around the area where Cayce located Atlantis—stretching from the Sargasso in the west to the Azores in the east—there have been several tremors and earthquakes in the scattered group of islands there; in February 1964 islanders from Sao Jorge fled in terror from the horrendous quakes that were starting. At the same time a volcanic island rose from the sea between Sao Jorge and the adjacent Fayal Island.

A leading Russian geologist, Dr. Maria Klinova, reported to the Academy of Science of the USSR that rocks dredged from depths of 6,000 feet, 60 miles north of the Azores, gave evidence of having been exposed to the atmosphere around 15,000 B.C.—the approximate date that Cayce estimated for the break-up of the Atlantean mainland. Several surveys of the Atlantic in this century have revealed the instability of the ocean floor in the Sargasso area; in August 1923, for instance, the Western Union cable company discovered that in one place the floor of the ocean had risen two miles since the last soundings were taken 25 years previously. So if Cayce was right about the location of this lost civilization, his fantastic descriptions of the Atlantean technology and social structure have that much more validity. Cayce claimed that misuse of the natural power source caused the cataclysmic demise of Atlantis and split the continent into five continents.

The Atlanteans had harnessed the power of the sun, according to Cayce, with a magical firestone akin to the modern laser beam. (The laser was not invented until 30 years after Cayce had referred to it in his readings.) He maintained this firestone was housed in a dome-covered building with a sliding top. Its powerful rays could project across the whole continent; like the laser beam, this power could be used constructively or as a weapon of destruction:

"The influences of the radiation that arose in the form of rays were invisible to the eye but acted upon the stones themselves as set in the motivating forces, whether aircraft lifted by gases or guiding pleasure vehicles that might pass close to earth, or the crafts on or under the water."

Although Case used language that can hardly be regarded as accurately scientific, he seems to have had an instinctive knowledge of many of the later discoveries of physics, such as the antineutron particle discovered in the United States in the 1950s some thirty years after Cayce had predicted the existence of antimatter which had been used by Atlanteans as a weapon.

Indeed, one of the remarkable consistencies of his readings about Atlantis is his constant references, long before the Bermuda Triangle was identified as such, to the dangers of the misuse of a gargantuan energy source in this particular area of the world: "The raising of the powers from the sun itself to the ray that makes for the disintegration of the atom . . . brought about the destruction of that portion of the land."

You do not need to believe every word Edgar Cayce uttered about Atlantis to see that he perceived a great deal that was in line with what our investigation, using only modern scientific findings, had itself discovered; it seems entirely feasible that the strange energies which exist in the Triangle today may have had their origins far in the past and be merely remnants of a power which was once much stronger.

Indeed, Cayce believed that Atlantis had been destroyed not once but three times. Interestingly, he conceived the origin of Atlantis as being other-dimensional in that man was said to have existed as long as ten million years, but only in a spiritual, nonphysical form. At some unspecified date, these ethereal, bisexual "thought-forms" divided into the five races, which originated simultaneously: white, black, yellow, brown and red, the last being the Atlantean race itself. The red race developed rapidly in Atlantis, becoming more material and dividing into two sexes, thereby becoming materialistic and corrupted.

During this early period Atlantis was invaded by "those of the animal kingdom," and the nations of the world conferred on how best to deal with this animal menace. Explosives were developed to cope with "those of the beast form that overran the earth in many places" (a reference to dinosaurs, which are supposed to have died out 63 million years ago?). With these destructive forces, the Atlanteans began the practice of human sacrifice.

The first colonies went to the Pyrenees in this early period. Further migrations were caused by the sinking of a portion of Atlantis "now near what would be termed the Sargasso Sea," due to the Atlanteans' mishandling of the destructive forces at their disposal. At this period the Atlanteans already had "machines of destruction that sailed through the air or under the water," used gas balloons and elevators, and "radioactive forces."

Atlantean civilization then split into two disputing groups: people belonging to the Law of One, a pure race, uncorrupted by materialism, and the Sons of Belial, who were the opposite, obsessed by the pursuit of sex and power. It was they who developed the instrument made of crystals harnessing the sun's power, which seems to have overloaded, initiating a volcanic upheaval around 50,000 B.C. that split Atlantis into five islands.

In the second phase that followed, there was a continuation of the feud. This time the Sons of Belial developed the laserlike "firestone," as well as many technical devices—television, tape-recorders, X-ray and antigravity machines—before misuse of these forces brought about another destruction, followed by a migration of Atlanteans to Peru, around 28,000 B.C.

The final destruction of Atlantis. in which every sign of the islands vanished, was preceded by migrations to Egypt, the Pyrenees, and Yucatan. The Mayan and Egyptian civilizations were begun by these migrants, who preserved records of Atlantis in various temples, including the Great Pyramid.

In order to make what Edgar Cayce said credible (for in spite of what his supporters say there is a lot in his readings which is garbled and contradictory), you have to interpret them not as literal fact, but as symbols of a deeper truth. Thus the technological devices can readily be seen on one level as a development in Cayce's mind of the many inventions being put before the public in the thirties, but on another level as representing lost knowledge in general, and in the case of the "crystals" or "firestone," knowledge of an earth force capable of both good and harm, and perhaps partly electromagnetic in nature.

It is also possible to make a case for a single origin for the cult of pyramid-building, and before coming to a description of the priesthood that enshrined Atlantean-like secrets into the construction of the Great Pyramid, it is well worth looking at this. The similarities between pyramids in three separate cultures—Egypt, Mexico and Peru—are so striking that if Atlantis did not exist as a fact, then there must have been an extraordinarily psychic parallel development of early civilizations.

The London-based scholar Patrick Smith has written that "like the Egyptian pyramids, their American counterparts are also shrouded in mystery. Although several pieces of the jigsaw are missing, an overview of the pyramid cult on both sides of the Atlantic reveals amazing parallels between three apparently separate and independent civilizations."

He goes on to list the most intriguing:

1. *Geodetic location:* Both Egyptian and American pyramids reveal that their builders were exceptionally skillful surveyors. Systems of geodetic markers have been found near all three sites, indicating an underlying common purpose that involved calculating the orientation of the pyramids with great precision.

2. *Construction of pyramid complexes:* The pyramids were not isolated monuments, but were integral parts of ancient metropolises. At Giza, Teotihuacan, and Castillo, the pyramids formed

part of carefully designed ceremonial centers whose overall architecture and planning was essential to the position of the pyramid itself.

3. *Spiritual significance.* The belief in life after death was the basis of all three cultures, and their concept of immortality and infinity was enshrined in their structures.

4. *Superhuman stonemasonry.* Pyramid erection involved not only transporting vast amounts of stone from distant quarries, but incredible proficiency in piecing the blocks together without mortar. The Pyramid of Cholula (cubic capacity 38,820,000 cubic yards) is the largest building in the world, with the Great Pyramid (35,402,790 cubic yards) a close runner-up.

5. *Parallel history of development.* Archaeology shows that the pyramid builders all started with a simplified "step design" as a foundation. The design was then elaborated to include specific functions in the pyramid. Both the Castillo and Giza pyramids have three floors of dry stone masonry, with ventilating shafts running horizontally and vertically.

6. *Knowledge of astronomy.* The carefully oriented pyramids, with their geodetic markers, are part of proven astronomical alignments, and knowledge of the universe was unquestionably central to what the architects were trying to enshrine. At Chichen Itzá the sun's rays make a giant serpent, whose head is at the foot of the pyramid, appear to slither up and down the stairway twice a year, at the spring and autumn equinox.

7. *Independent growth.* Although apparently springing from a common source or idea, the three pyramid-building cultures all developed independently, but with such striking similarities as to

indicate an inherited tradition of wisdom that included astronomy and mathematics.

8. *Interior networks.* In all pyramids there is evidence of interior workings. Similarly shaped chambers and shafts have been discovered in Peruvian and Egyptian pyramids, even though their purpose is ostensibly different. At the Sun Pyramid of Teotihuacan, a complex underground system of tunnels gives further evidence of the importance of astronomical orientation.

Patrick Smith goes on to point out that the loss of vital hieroglyphs may prevent us ever knowing the full secrets of the knowledge originally known to the astronomer-priests who directed the construction of the pyramids. However, our investigation found that the placing and physical dimensions of the Great Pyramid of Cheops still has much to tell us. Even more than is the case with Stonehenge and the related megaliths, there is a large volume of literature suggesting that here, too, is an embodiment of secrets known to Atlanteans. It may also be significant that the first phase of Stonehenge and the Great Pyramid were built within a few years of one another. Perhaps both were designed, in their own ways, to assimilate and exploit a magnetic or other-dimensional force which has so far baffled modern science.

Certainly there are a number of rarely associated parallels between the two monuments. Sir William Siemens, the British inventor, noticed the prickling sensations of static electricity inside the Pyramid of Cheops; Francis Hitching has collected many instances of people feeling the same thing when placing their hands on the ancient standing stones. Many dowsers have found their rods twisting violently in the presence of the pyramid, just as happens in stone circles; the U.S. master dowser, Jesse Cameron, detected an energy field which he identified as an "energy of form."

There is a similarity, too, in the way that both builders used massive blocks of stone in order to create a minutely accurate astronomical observatory, a fact first noted at the Great Pyramid by Arab historians. George Barton, Professor of the History of Science at Harvard University, has written that the astronomical ability of Egyptian priests is proved "not only by their calendars, tables of star culminations, and tables of star risings, but also by some of their instruments such as ingenious sundials, or the combination of a plumb line with a forked rod that enabled them to determine the azimuth of a star."

The British astronomer Richard A. Proctor has gone even further, suggesting that the main purpose of the Grand Gallery was to provide these early astronomers with the equivalent of a telescope. The high narrow walls of the gallery are exactly positioned to a point on the meridian where observers could see the movements of the stars and note their transits; grids of bars across the observation slot, now missing, would have made it possible to trace the declination of a particular star.

Remembering Stonehenge, the question must again be put: why this obsession with the movement of the heavenly bodies? Was it because of a link with an energy that the astronomer/priests were trying to handle?

As with the Taylor/Hitching experiments on the megaliths, there is one fascinating yet enigmatic scientific hint that something beyond our knowledge is operating in the Great Pyramid of Chephren. Hoping to find a hidden, sealed chamber, a team of scientists from the United States and the United Arab Republic took millions of readings to measure the rate at which cosmic rays decayed as they passed through the pyramid.

They hoped that the pattern, analyzed subsequently on a computer, would show up any voids hidden within the fabric—the equivalent of an X-ray photograph of the interior. In fact, none appeared. But something else much more remarkable happened.

In 1968, after $500,000 and thousands of man-hours had been spent on the project, the tapes were analyzed on an IBM 1130 at Ein Shams University near Cairo. Hundreds of tins of recordings were processed—and all that came out were meaningless print-outs showing impossible diagrams of the pyramid's dimensions.

Tapes recorded day by day, which should have shown a consistent pattern, differed enormously. Even stranger, each time a tape was processed it threw up a different result.

Baffled, the leader of the project, Nobel Prize–winning physicist Dr. Louis Alvarez, ordered a different device to be put in the central base of the pyramid. Still the computer print-out was a jumble of impossible and anomalous symbols.

Dr. Amr Goneid, head of the Egyptian side of the project, went on record to the science reporter from the *Times* in London with one of the most unequivocal admissions ever spoken by a scientist of his caliber:

"It defies all the known laws of science and electronics . . . it is scientifically impossible. Either the geometry of the pyramid is in substantial error, which would affect our readings, or there is a mystery which is beyond explanation—call it what you will, occultism, the curse of the Pharaohs, sorcery, or magic—there is some influence that defies the laws of science at work in the pyramid."

It was later found that the geometry of the pyramid was *not* in substantial error.

Modern attempts to re-create pyramid energy, as described in the many instructional books and kits available commercially, have not been experimentally successful. As with many other tests of various forms of psychic energy, it has been peculiarly difficult to set up repeatable conditions in a scientific laboratory where it can be demonstrated without doubt that, for instance, razor blades sharpen themselves or plants live longer when subjected to pyramid power.

However, the anecdotal evidence is now very strong, and if it is to be believed, it seems to have its basis in the harmony of numbers and geometry built into the pyramid shape. That the pyramid-builders were intrigued by the theory of number is beyond doubt: cryptically embodied in the mathematical dimensions of the Great Pyramid is the formula for the gravitational force field of the Earth. Scientifically, too, it is perfectly respectable nowadays to suggest that matter is a form of energy, and that elements of matter vibrating harmonically at different frequencies act like an "atomic transmitter" which can be affected by the mass of a pyramid.

Did the astronomer priests in those times know more than we do now? In some respects, our investigation was forced to the conclusion that the answer is yes.

Intriguingly, the concept of a triangle (as in the

Bermuda itself) seems to have been fundamental to this knowledge; and once again there is a connection between the builders of the megaliths and the pyramids, both of whom seem to have incorporated their beliefs into their stone structures.

As well as being astronomical observatories, the stone "circles" of the British Isles are often, Professor Alexander Thom has discovered, not true circles at all; they are elliptical, or egg-shaped. These carefully laid-out designs are the result of including right-angled triangles in the geometry, often with whole numbers such as 3, 4, 5, or 5, 12, 13, or 8, 15, 17; the purpose, Professor Thom thinks, was to draw attention to the fact that π-22/7-cannot be expressed as a whole number. The Egyptians seem to have been similarly puzzled, for they included the value of π in the geometry of their pyramids (themselves, of course, a three-dimensional use of triangles).

The interesting thing about this numerological knowledge is that it was so fundamentally important that it was kept a secret from all but a handful of elders. When Caesar conquered the Celtic people of Britain, who had inherited the wisdom of the megalith-builders, he noted that their most sacred matters were not written down, but were memorized by their Druid priests during a period of study lasting 20 years. The same was true of the school of Pythagoras in the fifth century B.C., where none of the philosophy was recorded in writing by those originally participating. The Egyptians, as we have seen, built their secrets cryptically into their monuments. In fact, the value of π was not put on paper until the sixth century A.D. (by the Hindu sage Arya-Bhata).

Why was this?

Perhaps, simply, because the occult knowledge of numerology, and of the triangle that lay at the heart of it, was too dangerous to be let loose among the general public.

So far as the Bermuda Triangle is concerned, the occult significance of the word "triangle" is strikingly apparent. Whether or not most of the disappearances have taken place precisely within the area delineated by Puerto Rico in the east, the Keys of Florida in the west, and Bermuda itself in the north, or whether the danger area is a "lozenge" or a "squashed rhomboid," as some other investigators have suggested, there is no doubt of the incantatory power of a triangle; it has become, in fact, a form of shorthand, and appropriately so.

Throughout the ages, those wishing to summon up "spirits" or "the devil" have used the Triangle of Solomon—an equilateral triangle drawn two feet outside a circle. Faust used it in his ceremonies; so did Aleister Crowley, the most well known of recent occultists. The theory was that the outline of the triangle represented some means of control over the other-dimensional power sources through which materialization could take place, the whole experience involving complex ritual and ingestion of various hallucinogens.

But it is necessary to go right back to Pythagorean times to find the first exposition of the triangle tradition. The school of Pythagoras flourished for some 200 years after his death, then seems to have gone underground before emerging again to provide a large number of Greek and Roman scholars with the basis of their belief that the first principle of the universe was mathematical.

Niomachus, a Pythagorean of the first century A.D., elaborated the theory:

"All that has by nature with systematic method been arranged in the universe seems both in part and as a whole to have been determined and ordered in accordance with number; for the pattern was fixed like a preliminary sketch, by the domination of number pre-existent in the mind of the world-creating God."

The notion that the Bermuda Triangle is the entrance to a time-space void, where other universes exist in parallel, and materialization and dematerialization can occur, would not have seemed at all strange to these Pythagoreans.

They interpreted the triangle as representing *all time*—past, present, and future—and were followed by other philosophers who extended this vision to see the triangle as representing also *all space* and *all material substance* in the world.

According to this view, the triangle is the "substratum" of the universe, a plane of truth containing the "models" of all substances, persons, and ideas in all worlds and in all times. Plato, later, had similar thoughts with his ideal world of forms, where there are also models or forms of every entity—physical or mental—in the universe.

So there is a sound historical and philosophic tradition for anyone who wishes to pursue the idea that strange energies and disappearances take place in the Bermuda Triangle; indeed, these traditions are very much more long-standing than the supposedly "rational" view of modern scientific investigators who scorn the idea of the Triangle mystery and who are unable through the limitations of their training to accept the evidence that has now accumulated.

Our investigation was particularly struck by the "other-wordly" atmosphere that surrounds the uncomfortably large number of ghost ships and ghost-like disappearances in the Triangle, all of them only explicable in terms of this ancient philosophy where spirits arise from the dead and the living can be seen to vanish.

Shortly after the Chase family vault was abandoned in 1820, a British square-rigger was dashed to pieces on Great Isaacs Rock in the heart of the Bermuda Triangle. Only an infant survived. The British dispatched a crew to construct a lighthouse on the spot.

The work took more than a year, and toward the end of this period, at the time of the full moon, the crew refused to go on shore. They had become petrified by the sound of low moaning that occurred at nightfall and by the coming of a spectral vision known as "The Gray Lady of the Rock." According to the natives, she was the dead mother of the baby found on the rock, and she returned each month in search of her child.

When the lighthouse was completed, keepers refused to stay on the rock for more than a month at a time. Finally, a keeper who was also a lay preacher in his church performed a ceremony designed to reassure the Gray Lady that her child was safe and well. It worked. She was never seen or heard again.

But is there some permanent space-time aberration at that spot, which enabled the Gray Lady to appear in the first place and may still operate spasmodically when conditions are right? Such a theory is commonly held by psychic researchers to be a contributory factor in the appearance/disappearance phenomenon.

Subsequent generations of keepers managed to

keep the light burning on Great Isaacs Rock without incident—until the summer of 1969, when the two keepers on duty were Mr. Ivan Major and Mr. William Mollings. On August 4 of that year, both men simply vanished. Nobody has ever been able to find out why. Bad weather, as usual, has been the preferred official explanation. But these men were trained to cope with bad weather—it was at the heart of their job. Or did they desert? Again, an unlikely solution; both men were dedicated public servants whose lives, the inquiry found, gave no hint that they had anything to run away from.

If indeed they vanished, in an other-dimensional way, they were in a sense in good company. Tales of ghost ships in the Bermuda Triangle abound, and although some can undoubtedly be put down to storms and hurricanes, others seem to have a genuine air of vanishment. Who can explain away the case of the nameless schooner found drifting between Bermuda and the Bahamas in August 1881 by the schooner *Ellen Austin*, herself becalmed at the time? When Captain Baker went aboard, he found to his surprise that although the ship was undamaged, and fully stocked with provisions, nobody was in sight.

Captain Baker ordered part of his crew to man the ghost ship. Each vessel was to remain within sight of the other. However, a storm whipped up, separating them, and when it was over the ghost ship was nowhere to be seen.

Captain Baker and the *Ellen Austin* continued on course for three days before finally sighting the ship again. To their horror, they found that the skeleton "prize" crew had disappeared as mysteriously as the first; there was not even a sign that they had ever been on board at all—provisions were still untouched.

Once again, the captain ordered a new crew. Each man was heavily armed and warned to yell and signal at the first sign of something strange. A light mist and hazy weather enveloped the two ships as they drifted along their course, and then, quite suddenly, the ghost ship which had been no more than ten lengths behind the *Ellen Austin* vanished. No sign of her or her latest crew was ever found.

It is a disappearance story that closely parallels the recent case of the disappearing tug which skipper Don Henry had recounted to our investigation. Indeed, it now seemed that wherever we looked, the historical and the recent were drawing ever closer together toward a solution to the secret of the Bermuda Triangle.

CHAPTER SEVEN

"Other Worlds"

It is not just in the Bermuda Triangle that people disappear from the face of the Earth; historically, there are a number of documented occasions in which the "vanishment" has taken place literally in front of other people. Edition number 55 of *Cornhill Magazine* described the case of Benjamin Bathurst, a diplomat representing the British Government at the Court of Emperor Francis, who vanished before the eyes of his valet and secretary. One morning in November 1809 Bathurst was examining the horses that were to take the party back to Britain; he walked around to the other side of the horses and was never seen again.

A similar incident was noted by John Osborne in the *Journal of Psychical Research*. He reported that in March 1895 he heard the sound of horses' hooves behind him. He looked around to see a man having difficulty controlling his horse and quickly dodged out of the way. When he looked again, the sound of hooves having passed him, there was no sign of the man or the horse; a magistrate on the investigation committee declared he was convinced by Osborne's evidence.

Or there is the well-attested case of the Somerset cripple Owen Parfit, who vanished in 1769. Formerly notorious as a pirate, he had been immobilized by a stroke. He was placed one day in a chair outside his cottage by a relative, who went briefly inside the house to fetch something. When she returned she could see no sign of the crippled Parfit—all that was there was the chair he had been sitting on and the rug that had been wrapped around him. Nearby witnesses, working on the adjacent farmland, were certain that nobody had passed the cottage or that anything untoward had happened.

However these events are classified (as hallucinations or as genuinely other-dimensional disappearances), they certainly happened as far as the people themselves were concerned. In turn, the existence of these cases—there are at least fifty listed in the literature examining them—makes more credible such Triangle incidents as the discovery of the sailing vessel *Rosalie*, found abandoned in 1840 with no life on board except for a few starving cats and canaries, her sails still set and the crew apparently having left her only a few hours before she was seen; or the schooner *City Belle*, found deserted 300 miles southeast of Miami in December 1946 (for those who find coincidences a part of psychic happenings, exactly 74 years after the disappearance of the *Marie Celeste*, and one year after Flight 19 vanished), perfectly seaworthy with all equipment in place except the lifeboats; or the freighter *Rubicon*, found derelict in October 1944 and reported by two Coast Guard cutters to have nothing living on board except a dog.

Freak meteorological conditions—"supernatural" might be a better description—are also far more common than is generally thought, and occasionally linked with disappearances. The London *Times* of 13 January 1943 reported the strange experiences of two small girls near Clavaux, France. They were picking leaves from the ground when they saw stones starting to fall about them; the stones fell with an uncanny slowness.

They ran home to tell their parents, and the entire group returned to the place where the phenomenon had taken place. Again, the stones fell with the same characteristics—but this time accompanied by a violent upward air current into which the children were dragged.

It was described as a kind of vortex, *but only affected the children.* The parents, untouched by whatever forces were operating, were able to pull the children away.

Such incidents were collected and reported over a lifetime by the journalist and phenomenalist Charles Fort. His death came in 1932, long before the Bermuda Triangle was identified as in any way a strange area, but there is no doubt that had he lived he would have delighted in the many reports of UFOs, waterspouts, curious lights, spinning compasses, and so on.

The world that he described in his books is full of falls of frogs and fishes from the skies, of mis-

siles from the upper regions, of levitation, teleportations, phantom ships, and sea monsters—all
taken from reliable newspaper accounts of the
phenomena immediately after they happened.
Some of the objects people saw—for instance,
meteorites—have now been accepted by scientists,
although the idea of blocks of metal falling from
the sky was ridiculed at the time. Other aerial
objects such as huge ice-blocks are still mistrusted,
in spite of such well-observed cases as the lump
which fell at the feet of a lightning expert from
Britain's Electrical Research Association in Manchester on April 2, 1973. It smashed into many
pieces, and he picked up the largest lump that he
could carry and ran home to preserve it in his
refrigerator; subsequent analysis showed that it
was of a crystalline structure like no other kind
of ice known to science, and certainly had not
come from any man-made source like an airplane.

Fort suggested that there may be some aerial
gravity-defying fields of such objects floating above
the Earth's atmosphere; his general world view
was that there was a "flux and vagary to all things"
in the universe, that fact and fiction were constantly being eroded, and that there was a hidden
rhythm to all phenomena.

Our own investigation was similarly coming to
the conclusion that the distinction between "natural" and "supernatural" events was almost impossible to define; so many strange occurrences were
taking place in the shadowy half-world between
what scientists regard as proven fact and reports
of "impossible" happenings from reliable observers
that it was safest to regard both views as real.

For instance, Dr. Jurgen Richter at the U.S.

Navy Ocean System Center near San Diego demonstrated to us how radar screens can sometimes mislead inexperienced operators into imagining that they are picking up a land mass, when what is truly being shown is a "ghost" anomaly known as Clutter Rings, caused by a particular set of atmospheric conditions. "No known vapor mass has ever been recorded on radar," he told us confidently.

However, the retired real estate broker Frank Flynn, for twenty years an officer in the Coast Guard, would disagree. He recalled for us with puzzlement an event that took place on an August night in 1956 on board the cutter *Yamacraw*.

"It was my first trip into the Bermuda Triangle. At the time of the incident, the weather was absolutely perfect. Sea conditions were flat and calm, visibility and ceiling just about unlimited. It was just a joy to be out that particular morning.

"At approximately one-thirty, on the midnight to 4 a.m. watch, we observed on the radar scope a solid line, giving us a reading about 28 miles away.

"We were a little concerned about it at first, as it had a strong resemblance to a land mass. However, a quick check of the navigation equipment indicated that we were right on course approximately 165 miles off shore. We tracked it, found that it was dead in the water.

"At that point I decided to call the Captain, who was Commander William D. Strouch, and I having been on the ship approximately two months it took him less than forty seconds to be out on the bridge. He surveyed the situation, rechecked the navigation, rechecked our position, checked all systems.

"Everything was normal. So we carefully approached it and practically an hour and a half later we got down to about half a mile from the radar target. At that point the Captain took command of the ship, started a gentle left turn so that we would not encounter this unknown object head-on, and we carefully moved closer to it. And we came down to within about a hundred yards from it. At that point we energized the 36-inch carbon arc searchlight and found that we were getting reflections off of the mass and the carbon arc just didn't seem to penetrate the mass at all.

"We moved even closer to it, again with the searchlight beamed on it, and there seemed to be little if any penetration. After doing this for approximately fifteen, twenty minutes we moved closer and cleared all personnel off the starboard wing of the bridge, and we sort of nudged it with the starboard wing, being careful to be able to pull right out again. We did this to it three times without incident.

"After that the Captain made a decision that we were going to penetrate the mass and continue on our way. So we circled around to the left, got back up to normal cruising speed and everybody entered the pilot house and we started our entry into the unknown mass.

"After penetrating we found that visibility was just about zero. It was just a strain, a real strange feeling to be going through this object. Shortly after we entered, the engine room called up and indicated that they were losing steam pressure.

"Now what was a situation of little concern became a situation of considerable concern at this point. As we started to reduce speed because of the loss of steam, the Captain became concerned and we were down to approximately four knots;

at that point he decided that we were going to come about and get out of there.

"As we started our turn that's when we broke out of the mass and we were on the other side. We estimate the mass was approximately half to two-thirds of a mile thick."

So many reports were now accumulating of electric, electronic, magnetic, and electromagnetic disturbances that our investigation decided it was time to take tally of them, both from the literature and from those reported directly to us by people such as Frank Flynn.

What emerged was, we felt, of great significance. Whereas the exact cause of any mysterious disaster can always be debated because the main protagonists are no longer alive, here was a powerful body of evidence that undoubtedly showed electromagnetic effects to be central in any solution. Most of the case histories can be regarded, we felt, as those of the fortunate crews—the ones who experienced the conditions for a near-disaster and escaped.

CASE 1. October 1492. Christopher Columbus and some of the crew on the *Santa Maria* saw a great "flame of fire" flash across the sky in the region of the Sargasso Sea. Earlier the crew reported severe disturbances in the compasses and the appearance of a mysterious light. Around the same time some of the crew also saw a mysterious light which gave the appearance of a candle being raised and lowered several miles away.

CASE 2. February 1928. Charles Lindbergh noted magnetic disturbances while flying over the Bermuda Triangle in the *Spirit of St. Louis*. Near the

Florida Straights both his compasses malfunctioned and the liquid compass card rotated without stopping.

CASE 3. July 1928. A plane on an air test route, a tri-motor, wooden-wing Fokker, was misdirected by a 50 percent compass variation and consequently could not locate land and crashed into the sea. The pilot and crew survived to tell the tale of the compass deviation and radio interference.

CASE 4. November 1943. Lieutenant Robert Ulmer noticed serious instrument malfunctioning when flying a B-24 over the Bahamas in good weather. Then the plane suddenly went out of control. The entire crew bailed out before the "wild" plane eventually crashed into a mountain.

CASE 5. March 1945. Commander Billson encountered major problems with both the radio equipment and the compasses as he was flying a Navy PBM over the Bahamas. Both the radio compass and the magnetic compass went around in circles, and the radio transmitter went dead. The instruments did not work until the plane reached its base.

CASE 6. December 1945. All the members of the doomed Flight 19 were dogged by instrument problems; none of their compasses were working as they should have been. The gyrocompasses were reported as "going crazy." None of the members of the mission were able to determine their position as the radio contact grew steadily worse.

CASE 7. July 1955. W.J. Morris, a veteran seaman aboard the *Atlantic City* witnessed the automatic steering device on the ship take on "a mind of its own." The ship was steering in a complete circle; at the same time Morris and an officer saw what appears to have been an incident of ball lightning. One compass was spinning at the time and the gyrocompass was completely inoperative. The navigation and electrical equipment aboard the ship never functioned again.

CASE 8. November 1964. Pilot Chuck Wakely noted a mysterious glow spreading across his plane on a flight through the Triangle to Miami, described as "a localized fuzzy light." When it appeared, both the magnetic and radio instruments started to malfunction.

CASE 9. July 1966. Don Henry, captain of salvage tug *Good News*, investigated disturbance on deck. Compasses spinning, engine failure. Line to barge being tugged was still taut, but barge itself had disappeared in clear weather. Line felt as if something tugging it. After about ten minutes, barge slowly reappeared in vision. Weather perfect and clear. All batteries on tug completely drained of power.

CASE 10. February 1968. On a flight from Nassau to Palm Beach Jim Blocker noticed severe magnetic aberrations in his plane's instruments. The radio flashed out, and the compasses started spinning. Most startling of all, the high-frequency direction finder also faded out. The aberration continued for the length of time that Blocker's plane was in the clouds.

CASE 11. December 1970. Bruce Gernon, Jr., an experienced pilot, was mystified by the strange formation of what appeared to be a "doughnut-shaped" cloud. He decided to fly into the cloud to investigate it. He found the formation to be massive, actually reaching down to the sea. At the same time the magnetic and electronic instruments on the plane ceased to work and he lost contact with radar control. When Gernon reached his destination, he found that he had "lost" 30 minutes out of the normal flight time for the trip.

CASE 12. March 1971. Aboard the USS *Richard E. Byrd* several of the crew members noticed the "legendary" malfunction of instruments during a cruise through the Bermuda Triangle. Walt Darling, an operations specialist on board, described how the crew lost radio communication, all the compasses went out, and the hazy sky prohibited taking bearings from the sky; many of the crew began to feel disoriented. After about ten days the ship regained contact with Bermuda, but the trip had taken four or five days longer than usual.

CASE 13. March 1974. On a voyage from Puerto Rico to the United States the crew members aboard the USS *Vogelgaing* noticed a strange loss of power throughout the ship. The electrical and mechanical systems broke down—even the ship's boiler ceased to work. At the same time, crew members said it felt like there was some invisible force field attempting to tear the ship apart.

CASE 14. April 1974. Passengers aboard the *Queen Elizabeth 2* experienced a mysterious power failure while the ship was cruising through the Bermuda Triangle. The entire heating and lighting system failed, and the passengers had to transfer to another ship. A Coast Guard cutter, the *Dakota*, reported the QE 2 had disappeared from radar at the time of its power failure. This report has since been denied.

CASE 15. August 1974. The appearance on radar of a mysterious land mass puzzled the personnel aboard the USCGC *Hollyhock*—they knew there was no land mass at the location indicated, yet repeated checking of the radar system revealed no faults there. Except for the mysterious land mass, everything was normal on the radarscope. Three months later the *Hollyhock* underwent a complete communications failure with one strange exception—the crew found they could communicate with the San Francisco Coast Guard Station way over in California. Both the incidents occurred not far from Miami Beach, and after several checks no defects were found in the equipment. a Cessna 172 across the Triangle to Haiti when the

CASE 16. December 1974. Mike Roxby was flying instrument panel and the radio transmitter went dead. He had to make a forced landing in Cuba; after taking off again, Roxby encountered the same trouble with the radio. This time the equipment failure was fatal. One of the surviving passengers described how a cloud appearing from nowhere coincided with the break-off in radio transmission.

CASE 17. December 1974. Pilot Jack Strehle was shocked by the appearance of a flashing blue light off the wing of his plane while flying over the Bimini area. At the same time Strehle noticed the magnetic compass was spinning wildly. Strehle was a commercial pilot, with considerable experience flying in the Triangle area, and was adamant that he had never seen anything like the light before.

CASE 18. July 1975. On a photographic expedition, Dr. Jim Thorne intended to take some film of an electromagnetic storm. Thorne pointed his camera at the horizon in the split second when a series of earsplitting thunderbolts exploded and lightning flashed across the sky. When Thorne developed the film he saw more than just a representation of the electromagnetic storm—an old-fashioned square-rigged sailing ship also appeared on the negative. There had been NO OTHER SHIPS IN THE AREA AT THE TIME. No one was able to explain this curious "electric apparition."

CASE 19. December 1975. The Coast Guard cutter *Diligence* suffered a total failure in radio transmission and navigation equipment while following up a report of a burning freighter. At the same time a mysterious green light "fell out of the sky" repeatedly. It was established that it could not have been a rescue flare, and when it was investigated there was found to be nothing there. A thorough check on the instruments of the *Diligence* found no obvious reason for the total malfunction.

CASE 20. August 1977. After taking off in a Piper Comanche, Bob Spielman found fuel gauges for both tanks read empty, although they had been checked three-quarters full on runway. Engine cut out. Right fuel tank suddenly registered one-third full. Engine re-started. On landing, not even vapor found in left tank.

Our investigation concluded that this large body of evidence concerning electromagnetic anomalies could not be ignored or brushed aside; somehow, the reported cases must contain the necessary clues that would lead toward our hoped-for discovery of the secrets of the Bermuda Triangle.

But a whole lot of questions still remained. What else was happening as well as electromagnetic disturbances? What could they signify, or lead to? Remembering our investigation's original criteria, why did they happen in the presence of just some people and in only some craft—why, in other words, were the anomalies in some way selective?

Spinning compasses on their own are not enough, in normal circumstances, to cause a disaster. They are simply a physical indication that something else much more serious is going on, or is about to happen.

Discovering what these things might be took us to the very fringe of scientific knowledge, into areas where even the scientists involved are uncertain about the outcome and implication of their work.

There is, for instance, the suspected but so far unproved link between electromagnetism and gravity, which in the words of one scientist is "waiting for another Einstein to give us the formula." The Canadian Government, as part of their research into this shadowy area of particle physics, found to their surprise that certain areas of "reduced binding" exist in the atmosphere.

Wilbur B. Smith, an electronics expert from Ottawa, led the research team and claimed to be able to detect these areas with special instruments that he had designed; they seemed to be roughly circular, with a maximum diameter of 1,000 feet, extending upwards from the surface of the Earth. They were not permanent—several circles of reduced binding were no longer at their location three or four months later.

Wilbur Smith found a close correlation between the areas and unsolved plane crashes. His contention was that the changed gravitational and electromagnetic fields might be responsible for the kind of extreme weather conditions that suddenly occur in places such as the Bermuda Triangle—conditions such as those described in the *FAA World* of October 1975:

> That there are unusual forces in the area is indisputable. The usually benign weather can change radically. A pilot may fly into a localized storm lurking under an apparently innocent nimbo-cumulus cloud, or into small hurricane-like storms, known locally as neutercanes, which may be imbedded in otherwise harmless rainstorms. The pilot flying in restricted visibility has no warning that he is headed towards disaster until it is too late. These cyclical storms pack a punch that can rip the wing off a plane and drop the pieces into the ocean where they will never be found.

Our investigation felt this was a likely solution to many of the Triangle mysteries—for instance, the disappearance of the Superfortress in December 1947 (listed as Case 5 in Section Three of Chapter Five), where the official verdict was that a tremendous current of air near a rising cumulonimbus cloud caused the bomber to disintegrate. In this case, and probably in others, an electromagnetic/gravitational force barely known to science had led to a "natural" disappearance.

Other reported effects of tampering with electromagnetic forces proved harder to track down. One such was the so-called Philadelphia Project, which the U.S. Navy flatly declares never existed, but rumors of which still persist after 35 years. In this, the aim was to create a strong magnetic field around a U.S. destroyer by means of electromagnetic generators in order to make it "disappear." A former high Navy official, now leading an oceanographic lab in Florida, tells the story:

"We use a very narrow portion of the electromagnetic spectrum where we can detect light and color, and which our eyes have adapted to. During the course of evolution we have come up with the ability to take the image from the eye and refine it into an image in the brain which we can relate to. Nobody knows exactly how this happens, and if you could interfere with the ability to process or even with the original transmission in that part of the electromagnetic spectrum, then all of a sudden you wouldn't be getting any of those wavelengths and you couldn't see what was there.

"I had no personal knowledge of the experiment, but I understand this was the aim, and the destroyer disappeared temporarily and the return was very successful."

As no eyewitness of the Philadelphia Experiment has ever been found, our investigation felt this theory could not be regarded as more than corroborative evidence. However, the thinking behind the experiment, whether or not it ever took place successfully, was exactly in line with our conclusion that the solution of some Bermuda Triangle disappearances must lie via electromagnetism in the direction of other forms of energy and probably other dimensions.

Until a few years ago, it would have been laughable to suggest this. Physicists as a whole were convinced that the four forces they understood and believed to be immutable (gravity, electromagnetism, the strong nuclear force that binds the atomic nucleus together, and the weak nuclear force involved in radioactivity) were sufficient to explain everything that happened in the universe. This is no longer so.

The Russian scientist Alexander Dubrov, for instance, believes he has discovered a new form of energy which he has called bio-gravitation. Through this he explains certain curious effects that occur during the process of cell division, when chromosomes move toward the poles in a manner inexplicable in terms of the known forces. He believes that this form of energy is but one of several waiting to be discovered, such as the way that high-frequency ultrasonic waves create physical effects, and that through them will come an understanding of psi energies.

At the same time, the work of a number of important physicists, notably Professor John Wheeler of Princeton University, has made it respectable to discuss seriously the possibility of other dimensions of space and time. Wheeler portrays a universe in continuous flux where superspace is a dimension beyond the space-time of Einstein's special theory of relativity.

He pictures this superspace as "a carpet of foam spreading over a slowly undulating landscape," in which bubbles constantly appear—the entrance and exit points which, in his theory, connect multiple universes. The crucial feature about multiple universes is that everything, living or inanimate, exists simultaneously, and that consciousness can cause a transition from one universe to the next.

So in superspace all points in time are accessible —past, present, and future. Strange appearances and disappearances are explained in terms of "journeys" between universes.

Professor John Hasted in London has made a logical development of this theory to take in other psi occurrences—the metal-bending, and the materialization/dematerialization phenomena which our investigation had found compellingly similar to observed behavior in the Bermuda Triangle (described in Chapter Four). The most relevant of his closely reasoned thoughts, read to a large audience at the Parascience Conference in London in September 1977, are included in an Appendix to this book.

Central to all these theories is the notion that consciousness, or intelligence, or "mind," can exist without physical matter, just as dreams or even ideas can; and that this implies a form of mental energy that can exist outside the confines of the universe that we are conditioned to recognize within a small band of electromagnetic frequencies.

This mental energy, it is suggested, can interact with the physical world to create matter—for matter itself is a form of energy.

Of course, for most people this is a difficult concept. But it is one that can be traced through many Eastern religions, and even as far back as Aristotle's division between body and soul. It is also one that many psychics have perceived as being the only model of the universe that makes sense. The Brazilian Hernani Andrades called it a "biological organizing model" in which life on our own world is activated. What we perceive are three dimensions of space and one of time; the universe of the biological organizing model must have at least four of space and two of time.

In this other world, according to Andrades, is all the knowledge of past, present, and future—and occasionally, an interaction with our own world gives an individual on Earth knowledge of this.

There is now a growing consensus, therefore, that our universe is not the only one; philosophy, religion, psychical research, and quantum physics point together in this direction. As John Hasted and others have pointed out, the possibility should not be denied just because it is difficult to comprehend, or because mainstream science has paid little attention to it until recently.

In the simplest terms, the undivided wholeness of the universe means that there is no "here" and "there," or "now" and "then," because the universe is in constant flux, each part of it in all time co-existing with the rest. All that we perceive is an infinitesimally small moment in time, in three spatial dimensions.

There is a modern photographic development which can illustrate this—the three-dimensional image called the hologram, or the "laser effect" of most good pop shows. Remove any small section from the holographic plate from which the image is produced, and the original structure of the subject can be reconstructed in its entirety from that one piece.

The idea of everything coexisting can also help with one of the most baffling of psi events: precognition. Right at the start of our investigation we noted how Eagle Bolotin and Alvin Kosnar had a premonition of disaster about Flight 19, and there have been many other examples since. Disasters, in fact, seem to be highly susceptible to prediction —especially, perhaps, at sea.

Fourteen years before the *Titanic* sinking, an ex-sailor, Morgan Robertson, wrote the *Wreck of the Titan*. Robertson conceived his stories in a state of trance and said they were the vision of his astral writing partner. Before he wrote the *Wreck of the Titan* he had a vision, recorded in Ian Stevenson's *Precognitions of Disaster*.

... he saw an immense ship ploughing through the icy waters of the mid-Atlantic in April. He could see the name *Titan* on its side, and the word "unsinkable" kept coming to him. In Robertson's vision the mighty ship rushed through the fog and hurled itself against an iceberg, and he heard nearly 3,000 voices raised in agonised screams.

The story, which used all the above details, was written in 1889. The *Titanic* sank in 1912. The eminent writer W.T. Stead also had a detailed premonition of the disaster, but that did not keep him from travelling on the ship and losing his life.

Teleportation, too, can readily be explained by the concept of "universe-hopping"—the person or object disappears temporarily into another dimension of space and time, of which naturally he or she has no recollection.

Our investigation was now forming its conclusion—an interim one, in the sense that scientific research into the subject is still in its infancy, but by the same token a conclusion that was as firm as could be made in the current state of knowledge. It was this.

Somewhere in the idea of quantum interconnectedness lay the answer to the most baffling of Triangle disappearances. Electromagnetic forces were involved, certainly as a warning mechanism through the disorientation of human beings and the malfunctioning of electronic and mechanical equipment; perhaps also, these forces were not just a prelude, but also a triggering device.

As to why the events seemed to be selective, the answer at last appeared to be, simply: They are no more or less rare than psychic events in the lives of ordinary people.

All of us, rarely, experience precognition or telepathy; perhaps, unrecognized, there are occasional psychokinetic events in all our lives, as well.

But if we foresaw the future all the time, or read the mind of anybody we cared to, or distorted metal objects at will—then, quite literally, we would not be living in the same universe.

Psi experiences, while an essential part of life, would interfere with our biological needs for survival if they happened too often; thus there is probably a biological "censor" on psi activity.

Similarly in the Bermuda Triangle, paranormal events happen only occasionally, *and select only those people who at that moment are biologically susceptible*. Almost certainly, it is the magnetic and climatic conditions in the Triangle that cause these events to happen more often than elsewhere.

It is now recognized by the most deeply thinking physicists that a new theory will be needed in the years to come to accommodate the phenomena that our investigation encountered. But a beginning has already been made.

It will be ironical, but by no means unprecedented, if the extraordinary interest that has been shown by ordinary people in the Bermuda Triangle, an interest which has simultaneously been derided by orthodox academic opinion, should turn out in the end to have provided the essential clues for a new way of looking at our world.

APPENDIX

"SPECULATIONS ABOUT THE RELATION BETWEEN PSYCHIC PHENOMENA AND PHYSICS"
J.B. Hasted, Birkbeck College (University of London)
(Extracts from paper read at Parascience Conference 2-4 September 1977, Imperial College of Science and Technology, London)

In the many-universe formulation of quantum mechanics, an infinite number of "universes" can co-exist in the same space, but without mutual physical communication. At the moment of an atomic transition the wavefunction does not collapse; rather, it splits into an infinite number of wavefunctions, each in its own set of space coordinates, and each differing from the others, for example in its energy. The observer, in a particular universe, in a different but incommunicable universe, would measure a different energy. . . .

The proposal inherent in the many-universe theory, that each atomic transition in our own insignificant bodies causes the remotest galaxies to split into an infinite number, has caused the theory to have only a very limited acceptance amongst physicists. It would be more satisfactory if bounds were placed upon the local universes. But such bounds could introduce physical effects akin to surface phenomena, and normal effects of this type are as yet unknown to physics. It is always assumed that the observer is in one universe, the same one as the observed phenomenon, and that each universe extends throughout the light cone.

But now we might speculate that the unconscious mind possesses the facility of receiving signals from, and hence of living in, a number of "universes." Since . . . physical signals cannot pass from one universe to another, we must assume that the unconscious mind is non-physical, but is able to communicate with physical reality. The mind is usually credited with the property of communicating with only one universe at a time; there are of course many different realities of mental existence within psychology (e.g. dreams) but even these are usually unique at any moment of time, so that it requires the passage of time for the mind to make the transition from one to the other. Since an infinite number of universes contain the physical body of a given individual, one might suppose that if telepathy exists, then some telepathic communication could be possible between at least some of the minds corresponding to those bodies. These communications would be equivalent to receiving signals from another "universe."

The speculation we make is that spatial boundaries could exist between local universes, and that certain minds are capable of perceiving (receiving signals from) several universes simultaneously, all the time unaware that they are doing so. Telepathically these minds can make contact with and instruct the minds of witnesses to receive these signals; their perceptions will then follow suit. . . .

Suppose that one mind is able to process signals from several universes, including the two on either side of a boundary; it would be unaware of the existence of the boundary or of its movement, except insofar as subsidiary physical effects such as metal-bending might result from the movement. Neighbouring minds (if indeed a non-physical mind can be said to have a spatial property) may not always concur instantly with the boundary movement controlled by the active unconscious mind; but after the boundary movement the active mind is in communication with the same universe or set of universes as are the neighbouring minds; otherwise the experimenter would not be able to observe the same physical effects as does the subject. At some moment all witnesses agree that they are in a universe in which the metal has bent. This is because there has been telepathic contact between these minds. Such contact may take time and be difficult to achieve; it may only be achieved retrospectively, in cases where the metal-bending is undertaken by a solitary subject.

In order to provide a framework within which the paranormal interface between mind and matter can operate, we have been forced to consider telepathic contact to be non-physical in origin; it is here assumed to be a property of unconscious minds, to be investigated by the methods of the information sciences rather than by the methods of the physical sciences; and nothing has been said about the precognitive and retrocognitive aspects of telepathic contact. We therefore are adopting a position of acceptance of the evidence for ESP and rejection of the hypothesis that it is an electromagnetic phenomenon. The more striking ESP phenomena, psychometric, precognitive or long-distance in character, are part of the justification for this rejection; another part is the telepathic information transmission rate, which has been supposed to be sufficiently large to rule out the ELF (extra-low frequency) hypothesis; again, the difficulties of conceiving the human frame as a tuned antenna, transmitting or receiving, are more than discouraging.

Although telepathic contact between non-physical minds has been assumed, it could be that minds are in fact physical, but operate at levels that are very weakly coupled to the material world. In the present theoretical framework the coupling would have to be sufficiently weak for telepathic transmission across universe boundaries to be possible.

Applications of parallel universe model

Teleportation. "Disappearance/reappearance events." The interpretation of teleportations, or "disappearance/reappearance events" from a parallel universe standpoint was in fact the starting point of our speculations. What is claimed in such events is that an object is instantaneously, or at least very quickly, transferred (for example, by a poltergeist subject) from one place to another. The author has witnessed more than fifty such events, but validation in a laboratory is very difficult. In a not inconsiderable proportion of these transferences there has been intervening matter, in the form of the wall of a room or of a box or capsule. Several transferences of electron microscope foils out of and into plastic capsules have been observed by us under good conditions.

It is not maintained that all poltergeist phenomena fall into this class of event; some flying objects are witnessed over their entire trajectory, and cannot be described as teleportations.

What is unacceptable to physics about disappearance/reappearance events is the implied passage of matter through matter. But no such difficulty arises once the participation of a number of different universes is supposed. Consider the apparent disappearance of an electron microscope foil from a capsule. Let the foil make a transition into a new universe at a certain time, whilst the capsule makes its transition at a later time. The occurrence of spontaneous atomic transitions at unpredictable times is one of the features of quantum theory. Before the capsule arrives in the new "universe" the foil may have, for a variety of reasons, moved out of or into the capsule interior, causing the illusion of matter through matter. But the entire capsule would have to be considered as a single wavefunction for such a large-scale transition to be possible. . . .

As before, it is necessary to postulate the ability of a subject telepathically to instruct the neighbouring minds to transfer their attention to a different universe, one in which an object takes up a different position from what is normal.

(After discussing the many-universe theory in

relation to metal-bending, and the phenomenon of "spirit" raps, Professor Hasted continues:)

It will be recalled that the levitation of furniture in some reported poltergeist phenomena must require a force several times beyond the capacity of the normal adult; the question is often asked, where does the necessary energy come from? To this we are able to give a consistent if not entirely revealing answer. On the many-universe theory, the total energy is (literally) infinitely greater than that available to a single universe. When furniture is levitated, the minds of the participants make the switch from a universe of lower potential energy to one of higher potential energy. The unconscious mind is providing not the energy but simply the information as to which universe they are in at which point in space. The force which lifts the furniture is of course the electromagnetic interaction, in the form of recoil of atoms when new atoms are created in positions which cause their orbitals to reorganise. . . .

Perception of a single or a combination of universes has been discussed as a mechanism for psychokinetic phenomena. We have no means of knowing, other than by single particle physics experiments which study a unique universe, just how many universes we live in simultaneously. One possibility is that the normal number is very large, and only becomes single locally for a short period of time during a particle experiment. The large number of universes need only differ each from each in very minor respects, but at certain moments the differences might become noticeable.

Consider the paradox that psychokinesis often seems to be markedly goal-oriented; the detail of how a subject brings about an event is not yet knowable, and may always remain relatively unimportant; notwithstanding that the refinement, the accuracy and the strength of metal-bending forces are surprisingly large, the subject has no detailed experience of the process, although he has a clear conception of the finished article he wishes to bring about. ...

A goal-oriented psychokinetic event much studied by Professor Rhine and his followers (and validated to a high degree of precision) is the throwing of dice. Subjects are able, using a randomly mechanical thrower, to influence the dice to follow, with greater than chance expectation, a previously given instruction. The detailed action required in this achievement would demand great skill (for example, if it is attempted with a magnetic die and hand-held magnet). But the goal presented to the subject is quite clear. All he must do is to perceive the correct choice of the six classes of universe presented to him. This choice may involve an element of precognition, but it would seem to present an easier task than that of manipulating the movement of the die. The many-universe interpretation may serve to reconcile the apparently goal-oriented processes with the classically simple movements of encased suspended pointers, superficially an entirely different psychokinetic process, but easily interpreted on the surface of action model. ...

The exercise of testing the ability of the many-universe hypothesis to explain other psychic phenomena is worth some thought. One particularly difficult, yet well-established, phenomenon is that which is sometimes known as psychometry. This is the ability of a psychic who handles a physical object to receive knowledge relating to its previous owner. It has always been difficult to find any relation between this phenomenon and the physical nature of the object; therefore the phenomenon has usually been taken to be purely mental.

What is the fingerprint that such objects carry with them? If it is physical, then perhaps a clue is to be sought in the molecular structure. There is, of course, sufficient information-holding ability in a crystalline or amorphous solid specimen, as is proved by the whole development of molecular memory devices. But the mechanism for imprinting such a memory physically presents great difficulties.

The boundaries between parallel universes may provide a more satisfactory mechanism for physical memory, rather in the manner of fibre optics. Suppose that boundaries enclose very fine fibres within which the universe content is different from what it is outside. If the diameter of the fibre is much smaller than that of an atom, then the physical effects of such a fibre will hardly be observable. These fibres may be imagined to stretch outwards from the original owner to the object, under the control of his unconscious mind. Nothing is known about what their length might be, but let us suppose that once they include one or more atomic nuclei within the object, they stretch without hindrance, so as always to maintain a link between owner and object. Such a link might conceivably last for years, provided that the physical effects were sufficiently small. It is a link between the object and the unconscious mind of the owner, so that a sufficiently sensitive psychic might be able to perceive, through it, the owner's unconscious mind. In some reported cases the owner is dead at the time of the perception, so that some interesting non-physical questions are raised. It would be a curious feature if a physical link were necessary in order that contact be made between two minds, which are themselves, according to our outlook, non-physical. Perhaps a physical link between unconscious minds is also involved in dowsing.

It is disturbing to think of these phenomena in physical terms; the entire world would have to be interlaced with myriads of fibres; yet, strangely, this interlacing, which is a feature of human thought, is not nearly so disturbing when it is regarded as non-physical.

THE BEST OF THE BESTSELLERS
FROM WARNER BOOKS!

BIG STICK-UP AT BRINK'S! by Noel Behn   (81-500, $2.50)
Hailed as "the best book about criminals ever written." BRINK'S
recreates a real-life caper more exciting, more engrossing than any
crime novel. It's the most fun you can have from a bank robbery
without taking the money!

PASSION AND PROUD HEARTS   (82-548, $2.25)
by Lydia Lancaster
The sweeping saga of three generations of a family born of a great
love and torn by the hatred between North and South. The Beddoes
family—three generations of Americans joined and divided by love
and hate, principle and promise.

SUMMERBLOOD by Ann Rudeen   (82-535, $2.25)
The four exquisite women of Land's End . . . sweet with promise
. . . wild with passion . . . and bound forever to one lonely man
tortured by his terrible past. A big, lush contemporary novel hot
with searing sexuality.

THE FAN by Bob Randall   (82-471, $2.25)
A masterpiece of humor, suspense and terror as an aging Broad-
way actress is pursued by an adoring fan whose obsession with love
and death leads him deeper and deeper into madness. A **New York
Times** bestseller, Literary Guild Alternate, Reader's Digest Con-
densed Book, and serialized in **Photoplay.**

 A Warner Communications Company

IN 1942 THE U.S. RATIONED GASOLINE

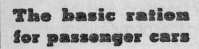

The basic ration for passenger cars

A DRIVERS
MUST DISPLAY
THIS STICKER

That was wartime and the spirit of sacrifice was in the air. No one liked it, but everyone went along. Today we need a wartime spirit to solve our energy problems. A spirit of thrift in our use of all fuels, especially gasoline. We Americans pump over 200 million gallons of gasoline into our automobiles each day. That is nearly one-third the nation's total daily oil consumption and more than half of the oil we import every day . . . at a cost of some $40 billion a year. So con serving gasoline is more than a way to save money at the pump and help solve the nation's balance of payments, it also can tackle a major portion of the nation's energy prob lem. And that is something we all have a stake in doing . . . with the wartime spirit, but without the devastation of war or the incon venience of rationing.

ENERGY CONSERVATION - IT'S YOUR CHANCE TO SAVE, AMERICA

Department of Energy, Washington, D.C.

A PUBLIC SERVICE MESSAGE FROM WARNER BOOKS, INC.

The MS READ-a-thon needs young readers!

Boys and girls between 6 and 14 can join the MS READ-a-thon and help find a cure for Multiple Sclerosis by reading books. And they get two rewards—the enjoyment of reading, and the great feeling that comes from helping others.

Parents and educators: For complete information call your local MS chapter, or call toll-free (800) 243-6000. Or mail the coupon below.

Kids can help, too!